BARE
NECESSITIES

Essential LIFE skills
for surviving
in the REAL world

Jemma Wayne

PIATKUS

Visit the Piatkus website!

Piatkus publishes a wide range of bestselling fiction and non-fiction, including books on health, mind, body & spirit, sex, self-help, cookery, biography and the paranormal.

If you want to:
- read descriptions of our popular titles
- buy our books over the internet
- take advantage of our special offers
- enter our monthly competition
- learn more about your favourite Piatkus authors

VISIT OUR WEBSITE AT: www.piatkus.co.uk

Copyright © 2005 by Jemma Wayne

First published in 2005 by
Piatkus Books Ltd
5 Windmill Street
London W1T 2JA

e-mail: info@piatkus.co.uk

The moral right of the author has been asserted

A catalogue record for this book is available from the British Library

ISBN 0 7499 2636 8

Text design by Goldust Design
Edited by Jan Cutler
Illustrations by Megan Hess and Rodney Paull

This book has been printed on paper manufactured with respect for the environment using wood from managed sustainable resources

Data manipulation by
Action Publishing Technology Ltd, Gloucester, GL1 5SR

Printed and bound in Denmark by
Nørhaven Paperback A/S, Viborg

CONTENTS

ABOUT THE AUTHOR

Jemma Wayne graduated from Cambridge University in 2002 before studying journalism at Westminster. She worked for a year as a reporter at *The Jewish Chronicle* before returning to her first passion – books. As well as *Bare Necessities*, she has also recently completed two novels and is midway through a third. She is a keen athlete and lives in North London with her husband James.

For the Waynetrain and my wonderful
husband James – my bare necessities.

ACKNOWLEDGEMENTS

I am greatly indebted to the following people, who
provided invaluable advice and without whom *Bare
Necessities* would be very bare indeed:

James, Sammy and Dan Kattan, and all the boys at
  Squires Estates
Alper Alkan
Amanda Cline at S&G Recruitment
Dani at Trim Rims
Graham, Michael and Mark at Shenley Garage
Charan Shetty at NatWest
Sonal Sachdev
Tania Gold
Damian Collier

And most of all, my mum, Geraldine – a constant source
of wisdom, and a woman who always knows the answer
to any question that starts, 'Mum, what do I do if ...'

INTRODUCTION

So, you've passed your A levels, you've left home, you know exactly how trigonometry works and who wrote the *Odyssey* ... and then someone asks you how to switch on the washing machine. When finally you give up and drag your smelly undergarments off to the launderette, your car gets a flat. And when your detailed knowledge of *Grease* fails to see you through the tyre-changing process, the AA man arrives and asks for a cheque, which you suddenly realise you've never had to write before. Eventually, your mum arrives, pays the man, who by now is shaking his head in disbelief, and takes you home just in time for you to rush to your first shift at the new pub. Then the manager asks you for your P45 form.

You envisage yourself in a comic strip with a huge speech bubble coming out of your panicked head, saying, '*?WHAT?!*' No one told you about a P45 form. What is it anyway? Is it a code for some incredibly obvious thing that you *must* know about because the manager's looking at you as if you've just landed on Earth from the planet Ug? All at once, you feel like you've been shoved on stage in front of thousands of people and you haven't learnt your lines. You're supposed to be a grown-up, but nobody's shown you how!

Of course, there are some people in life who do know how. They're rather an annoying smug kind of person who seems to have had access to some secret manual of life skills. For them, everything happens as planned: once out of the womb, they instantly make cooing sounds; at two they're terrible; at five, precocious; on hitting 13 they immediately dye their hair and hibernate in their bedroom; by 16 they have grandiose ideas about changing the world; and by 18, or at most 21, they're entirely ready to be a grown-up. Intuitively, they know how to do things. They know exactly where to go, precisely who to call – and they do it loudly, so that we all know just how self-sufficient they are.

The rest of us, however, stumble out of school or university bleary-eyed and reluctantly dusting away the remnants of childhood. We have a degree, but not a clue; exam results, but no laundry training; perhaps even a highly paid job, but no idea how to mortgage a house with our savings. We feel like we're playing dress-up, and at any moment we'll be spotted as simply a kid, trying to pass himself off where he obviously doesn't belong – in the adult world.

Now, we should pause for just a minute on the fact that this is not entirely our fault. Yes, we were taught how to use computers and we understand the finer points of genetics, but we didn't have home economics at school. We never learnt dusting, we didn't do tax, and as far as I remember, changing a wheel was not on the A-level syllabus. OK, so we could have nagged our mums to teach us how to cook, and asked our dads for regular lessons about how to fill in tax returns ... but, come on, we were kids, there were better things to do!

So, blame being properly attributed, unfortunately there remains the task of catching up. We have to learn *how* to be a grown-up, *how* to master the skills that those irritatingly smug people seem to possess already. Like a lost art, adulthood has to be carefully brought to life, explored and conquered. But how can we do it? Where do we find it?

The answer is: right here – all the bare necessities, laid out nicely for you; a manual of life skills that is not so secret. Read. Grow. Learn. Live (... then seek out a person of the smug variety and loudly shout: 'Ha Ha! I can do it too!').

1
FOOD SURVIVAL: 21ST-CENTURY CAVEMAN

Surviving in the 21st-century cave that is the high-tech kitchen can be a daunting experience for many live-alone novices. And preparing food that other humans find edible is the biggest challenge of all. The first time I decided that I was mature enough and a big enough culinary whiz to share my genius with the public was on the eve of my very grown-up sister's wedding, for eight extremely hungry relatives just flown in from America. By this time, I'd already been cooking my way through university for two years, and while I knew I wasn't yet quite in the league of Nigella Lawson, I was certain that I was well past the era of beans on toast. In fact, I had even developed a number of specialities. So, eager to tickle the taste buds, I decided that pasta would be just the ticket – or, Fettuccine Fromage à la Jemma, to be exact.

Now, I'd cooked pasta many times before. I'd already overcome the trials of it being too hard or too sticky, the sauce too thick or too runny, the twirls too soft ... or too irreversibly attached to the inside of the pan. But the one thing I hadn't encountered before was the challenge of cooking for more than two people. OK, I know it doesn't sound like rocket science, but I had in my head a well-established idea of how much pasta was needed for one person, or for two, but beyond that was a complete blank. Of course, I could have measured the amount for two people four times, which any four-year-old worth his salt will tell you would equal pasta for eight. But no, I thought I'd be fancy. I turned the pasta pack over, glee-fully discovering a recipe for fettuccine that served two, and used four packs of pasta to make enough for eight. It was only after I'd filled three huge serving bowls with enough pasta to feed at least 20 people, that I read the fine print at the bottom: 'This pack contains six servings'. I'd made enough pasta to feed an army. We had pasta coming out of our ears. And it didn't even taste that nice. It made a good joke at the wedding the next day.

But never fear, this is not a rite of passage. There are ways to conquer the kitchen. There are means to avoid such food faux pas.

Machinery – conquer the beast

The first and most important element to become familiar with in the kitchen is your machinery. It's no good understanding the finer points of basting and rolling if, when the cookbook tells you to 'preheat the oven to 240°C', you don't know how to switch the damn thing on. All kitchen appliances vary, so it's impossible to give a highly detailed explanation of each one, and the best but very boring solution is to read the manual. But don't worry, they're not as complicated as they may seem:

THE HOB

This is where you will do a high percentage of your cooking. Everything happens here from frying to poaching, boiling to steaming, and from fancy flipping to cooking animal, vegetable and mineral in the catch-all and absolutely indispensable miracle that is a wok. The first task is turning the hob on.

NB: before even approaching the hob itself, locate your electricity isolation switch. This will probably exist

somewhere on the wall in the kitchen and needs to be turned on to make sure your electricity supply is actually reaching the hob to spark the flame on a gas stove, or heat up the plates for an electric stove. Once this has been done, you're ready to look to the hob itself.

All gas hobs are different, but usually they require a combination of turning a knob and pressing a switch to ignite the flame. Sometimes, this is combined in one knob in an elaborate press-and-twist action that would seem better suited for the circus than the kitchen. But bear with it – a bit of practice and you will soon be a hob-high-flier, available for weddings, christenings and bar mitzvahs. Electric hobs, however, are more straightforward, and simply turning the knob will heat up the plate.

Most hobs will have four rings of varying sizes. This is not for the sake of art. Each size of ring is suited to a different task, depending on what you are cooking and what size pan you are cooking with. Usually, the rules are fairly straightforward: if you're using a large pan, use a large ring. This will ensure that the whole contents of the pan are heated evenly, instead of burning the food in the middle where the smaller rings concentrate heat, and remaining cold at the edges. Similarly, if you're using a small pan, use a small ring. This will prevent the heat from craftily escaping around the edges of the pan and heating (or burning) only the side of your pan, instead of the food within it. Of course, some stoves have more than four rings, which means you can tailor your choice more finely and cook lots of delightfully different dishes all at once. Others, however, have just one. In this latter case, try not to feel cheated, but, instead, think Hobbit: one ring to rule them all! And remember, size isn't the only thing that matters.

It is also important to consider the strength of the heat (especially in the case of gas hobs where you have a naked flame). Turn it too high, and the outside of the food will cook too quickly, rapidly resembling a lump of charcoal, while the inside remains raw enough to give you food poisoning. It could also burn, stain and/or melt the pan, not only destroying your cooking tools, but also risking poisoning your food with liquid metal and forcing you to take a trip to the hospital ... or at least to the toilet. However, turn it too low and the food will take forever to cook, making some things too hard, others too soggy, and others that simply refuse to crisp. There's no fancy trick to overcome this – it is an interminable battle and largely a process of suck it and see. Usually, however, as a rule of thumb, it's a good idea to start on a high heat if you are bringing water up to the boil (such as for pasta and boiled potatoes); for other things start with a medium-low flame and adjust as logic dictates. (Yes, I know this means actually watching the cooking process and not disappearing into the living room to watch *Hollyoaks*, but don't forget that the hob is our 21st-century caveman way of starting a fire, and flames shouldn't generally be left unattended – unless you have no need for a roof over your head, and very good insurance.)

Electric hobs, which have no flames, will reduce the risk of causing a fire and/or burning your pans. However, without a flame to act as a giveaway there's the extra issue of making sure the hob is off and completely cool before you place anything on it, such as a plastic bag or box, the dishcloth, or your hand.

....

NB: Electric hobs are slower to heat up and cool down, and more difficult to control than gas hobs, but they are far easier to clean and manage. There's also a range of new technologies for electric hobs (such as induction heating and halogen zones) that can speed up the heating/cooling process, and even increase safety by becoming hot only when in contact with a pan.

....

Some cautions

- Electric hobs are not the only ones accidentally left on. Even with gas hobs it's possible to overlook a burning flame, or even worse, a hob that's on but not burning. In cases such as this, instead of cooking your food, the gas is leaking out into the room doing its best to suffocate you, or waiting to explode just as you're preparing to relax into a candlelit bath. So, no matter how obvious it sounds, ALWAYS make sure the stove is switched off. And if you find yourself lying in bed with the sneaky suspicion that you've accidentally left it on, don't play it down as nothing and overlook it until morning, after all, you do want to wake up in the morning. Drag yourself out of bed and check it! Of course, if you find yourself having these thoughts night after night, and after checking the stove you discover that you're not simply very forgetful but seem instead to be contemplating your own doom, perhaps seek further advice ... like from a health professional.

- Be careful about what you leave by the hob. You may think you have conquered all obstacles (you've got the stove lit, on the right ring, with the right level of flame, and you're even using a wooden spoon to stir instead of a metal one that will heat up, burn your hand, or melt), but there's a couple more things to consider. NOTHING except the food itself should be left in the pan while it is cooking. And nothing should be left leaning on the pan either. Spoons can slip, tea towels can fall, objects can burn. Remember: man make fire!

THE OVEN

Once the king of kitchens everywhere, in recent years the oven has suffered a demotion, following the advent of microwaves and take-out food. However, it's still an essential for many of the traditional favourites, and come Christmas Day, few people try to microwave a turkey. So, let's turn that oven on!

There's not a lot that can go wrong at this point. If there's a power button, press it; if there's a knob, twist it; if there's a dial, turn it from 'off' to 'on'.

OK, perhaps I'm oversimplifying just a little. There are a few more options than that – temperature, for example. Everything has a different cooking time, and cookbooks or the instructions on the back of the pack are your best reference point. However, if in doubt, remember that 180°C/350°F/Gas Mark 4 is a pretty average temperature for most foods, or use a little higher temperature for pastries and veg.

....

NB: recommended cooking times assume that the oven is starting at the specified temperature, so remember to pre-heat your oven before you start.

....

Now you're ready to cook. Open the oven door and place the food item onto the oven shelf, remembering to don a pair of not necessarily very attractive but thick and protective oven gloves. Make sure that if the food is in a container it is a purpose-made ovenproof one. Plastic bowls must NOT go in the oven. Nor should saucepans, chopping boards or your best china. Ceramics, Pyrex glass, or other ovenproof dishes are the best-suited materials for oven cooking. Or, if you don't have any of these, a piece of foil on top of the oven shelf will do the trick for cooking food such as pizzas or reheating pies or flans.

The next question, of course, is which shelf to put it on. This varies a little depending on the oven. For example, convection, or fan-assisted ovens spread the heat evenly around the oven, keeping it at a fairly even temperature. However, most ordinary ovens heat from the top, which means that the top shelf is generally much hotter than the others. This will affect your cooking time and is important to monitor so that you don't get a roast chicken that's crispy on the outside and still sporting salmonella in its cold innards. But never fear, cookbooks will usually tell you which shelf to place things on, and some general rules are: meat and veg on the middle shelf, cakes and pastries on the top.

The final hurdle to cross when using the oven is the question of blind faith – a delicate balance between your extrasensory knowledge of how the potatoes are doing, based on years of culinary experience (and the reading of this book), and the desperate urge to check on them, just to be sure. Most ovens have glass doors so you can get a distant view anyway, but if you're forced to check on your meal (and in some cases you will have to turn, test, or flavour the food) try to open the oven the absolute minimum number of times. Every time you open the door, the temperature inside the oven drops by around 25°C/80°F, which not only will increase your energy bill, but will also alter your cooking time, throw the potatoes out of whack with the fish you're frying on the hob, unbalance the entire synchronised process that was your dinner, and cause you to have a nervous breakdown. Or, in the case of normal people, it might mean your fish will be a bit cold.

Of course, as with everything, there are exceptions that upset the norm and make everything far more complicated. In the case of ovens (or at least ones that have the grill as part of the main or top oven), when grilling, it's often advised to leave the door open.

THE MICROWAVE

Ah, the saviour of teenagers, men, and busy mums everywhere! The microwave has revolutionised cooking so that even the most inept of chefs can concoct a gourmet delight – with the help of Marks and Spencer and two-and-a-half minutes of zapping. And for the computer generation, raised on a staple diet of digital technology, nothing could be easier. Simply put the food into the microwave and type in the time you want to zap it for. Press 'cook' or 'start', wait till it pings, and remove. Voilà!

For defrosting, do exactly the same, but press the 'defrost' button before the time (or, for some microwaves, after the time – try it out and see).

For reheating, it's the same rules again. In fact, there are just two troubleshooting areas to consider. First of all, the time you heat things up for. As always, each food is different, but almost all food products will give you instructions on the back as to how long it should take to reheat them in a microwave. Some will give you choices such as 'for a 600W microwave cook for 3 mins' or 'for an 800W microwave cook for 2 mins'. Don't panic. This is not the start of an algebraic equation. It is simply a way of tailoring instructions to fit the strength (or wattage) of your machine. Just look at the front of your microwave for the number that is followed by a W (usually somewhere at the top or bottom), and see what wattage your particular machine is. Alternatively, if for some reason you can't locate this number, go for the lower time given on the instructions and then add another minute or two if the food isn't cooked enough. Some microwaves will help you out even further and come pre-programmed with auto-cook or auto-defrost buttons for various common items such as meat or veg. If you're lucky enough to have one of these cooking 'speed-dials', you may never have to think in terms of numbers again. Simply press 'cook' or 'defrost', select the appropriate auto-programme, and wait. However, if you find yourself at a complete loss, with no auto-button, and no cooking instructions to help you, remember that microwaves generally cook in terms of minutes, not hours, so plugging in 2 mins and then taking a look is usually a good rule of thumb. (Alternatively, cooking for an hour and then checking is a good way to blow up the kitchen.)

The second problem zone is the container that the food is in. Most microwave meals will come in a microwaveable container, so you can just pop it in and go. However, some food providers are craftier, with a taste for morbid humour. On the front of the handy container they will shout something like, 'Vegetable lasagne. Microwaves in 2 mins!' But in tiny writing on the back it will remind you to transfer the contents from said container before placing in the microwave – not so handy. This is because some containers will burn or melt or explode, or all three.

....

NB: metal should NEVER go in the microwave – this includes foil and the sneaky metal rims on the edge of some plates. Paper should also never enter the zapping zone. Some plastics are OK – if they specify that they are microwave-safe – but plastic containers designed for cold storage will melt and leak toxins into your food. You are safest with Pyrex glass, china and other ceramics, which, fortunately, is what most crockery is made of.

....

A final thought on microwaves: make sure there is something in it before pressing 'cook'. OK, this may sound obvious. I mean, why would anyone want to cook air? But you'd be surprised at how tempting it is to get the microwave going and watch it spin when you're bored – or drunk – in the kitchen. This, however, is another no-no, likely to make your machine explode. Besides air, other items that don't sit well in a microwave include gloves, underwear, plants, dogs, cats, and anything else that moves.

OTHER APPLIANCES

There is a whole plethora of other appliances out there that can be used for cooking. Some are self-explanatory and I'll presume that even the most kitchen-inept can conquer those on their own (the kettle and toaster, for example). Others are more complicated but there are far too many to describe, with new ones being invented all the time. In fact, some people have even started using old appliances for new things, such as trout à la dishwasher and spinach à la washing machine. These, of course, are not recommended, and, while possibly making your meal the talking point of a dinner party, could have disastrous consequences ... like a very fishy load of laundry.

However, a couple of my personal favourite additions are: the rice cooker – this can be filled with a variety of ingredients, and makes just about the best rice in the world; the cappuccino machine – expensive, but quickly recouped in a diminishing number of visits to Starbucks; and the George Foreman Grill – on which you can cook practically anything, and healthily too!

Cooking dictionary – the bible

Once you've mastered the machinery, you're ready to go, and if it's cheese on toast you're after, you can probably stop reading here. However, if you're shooting for anything more complicated than that, and the instructions on the back of the pasta that say 'bring to boil then allow to simmer' are confusing you, read on.

The basics

Get to know the basic techniques and remove some of the mystery from cooking.

BOILING

To boil: fill a pan (not a frying pan, but a proper saucepan with tall sides) with water and place on the hob (remembering to find an appropriate-sized ring if possible). Usually recipes or packet instructions advise to 'lightly salt' the water. This simply involves sprinkling a little salt into the water – a little; we're not recreating the Dead Sea here. Turn on the hob and then wait until the water starts to bubble. It has now boiled.

....

NB: to speed up this process, place a lid on top of the saucepan so that the heat isn't lost, or boil the kettle first and then pour this pre-boiled water into the pan. Bring the water back to the boil on the hob.

....

Once boiled, you can place the food into the pan. (Carefully: plopping potatoes into the pan from a height of 60 centimetres while you pretend you are an artistic culinary genius, can easily leave you with scars all over your arms and face from splashed boiling water – not so clever.)

If the instructions simply say 'boil' or 'bring to the boil', this means that the water should continue to bubble throughout the cooking process and you will need to keep the hob on a medium-high flame. However, if the instructions tell you to 'simmer', this means that the water should remain just below boiling (or bubbling) temperature and you will need to turn the flame down low. If you are instructed to 'bring to the boil and then simmer', this means you should heat the food on a medium-high flame until the water with the food in it is bubbling, then turn the flame down so that it can simmer (this is when the water is just boiling but barely moves).

Some foods, of course, don't need water and can boil in their own juices. The general rule is: if it's a solid, add water; if it's a liquid, or has quite a bit of liquid in it, don't.

....

WARNING: foods that are being boiled can reach boiling point very quickly and very suddenly. Sometimes the bubbles become so vigorous that they start rising up and flooding out of the pan. This is annoying if it is water. It's a nightmare if it's anything else – think bits of tomato soup splattered over the hob, walls, ceiling, floor, and, by the time you reach the knob to turn it off,

you. This can happen even when pans are left on the very lowest of simmer, so remember to keep on eye on everything you are cooking, and if you notice bubbles starting to rise up, jump into action and turn that flame down.

....

How to boil an egg

Master this simple and basic skill, and you can have a quick snack or breakfast in minutes.

- If you have an 'egg piercer,' use it to make a hole in the larger rounded end of the egg (this is where there is an air pocket; by piercing the shell you allow the air to escape rather than exploding the egg as the air expands).
- Put the egg into a small pan with cold water to cover.
- Put on a high heat and bring to the boil.
- As soon as the water is boiling, start to time it. It will take about four minutes for soft-boiled eggs, six minutes for medium-boiled eggs and 10 minutes for hardboiled eggs. If you are hardboiling an egg, take it out of the boiling water as soon as the time is up and plunge it into cold water to stop it from continuing to cook in the shell.

FRYING

OK, we're at the hob again, and you're in luck because frying is possibly the easiest of all cooking methods. It's quick, simple, and easy to monitor in case it all starts going wrong. So, here we go:

Place a frying pan on the hob. Pour in a little (a teaspoon or two) of vegetable oil/olive oil/margarine/ butter, and turn on the hob. Wait for about 30 seconds for the oil or solid fat to warm up or melt, and then place the food in the pan. You are now frying!

Just make sure that the flame isn't so high that the oil starts spitting at you. And make sure that you turn the food regularly, to ensure that it's cooking evenly and not sticking to the pan.

NB: food is more likely to burn and stick to the pan if you use butter alone, so it's a good idea always to add at least a dash of oil. The type of oil you use is pretty much down to personal choice, although olive oil and vegetable oil are the most common. Vegetable oil is a good, general-purpose and inexpensive cooking oil, but olive oil has traditionally been seen as healthier because it is a monounsaturated fat instead of a polyunsaturated one. However, don't use extra virgin oil for frying.

Deep-frying is really the same process as frying, except that the pan is deeper and much more oil is used. You will also need some special equipment, such as a frying thermometer and tongs. The first step is to half-fill the pan with oil. For deep-frying, vegetable oils or peanut oil are best because they have high smoking points – and you will be frying at a high temperature. Turn on the hob and heat the oil until the temperature has reached approximately 190°C/375°F. Using the tongs (or a frying basket if you have one) slowly submerge the food in the oil until it is completely covered. (Beware that the oil will spit, so dunk the food in slowly, withdrawing it if the oil starts to boil up.) Leave it to cook until golden brown, remove, drain the excess oil on paper towels, and serve.

Always be careful when using deep fat. If the pan catches fire, turn off the heat source if it is safe to do so. Carefully cover with a British Standard fireblanket, if you have one. Do not move the pan, but leave the kitchen and call the fire brigade immediately. NEVER pour on water, as this will create a powerful fireball that will set the whole kitchen alight.

....

WARNING: when you have finished frying, NEVER rinse the pan immediately as the water can cause any remaining hot oil to spit up at you and burn.

....

STEAMING

As steaming is a healthy way of cooking that can be used for a variety of dishes from fish to veggies, it's a good method to learn, and it's easy too. We're still at the hob and the first thing you need to do is boil a saucepan of water. Next, place a steam basket (if you have one), or a sieve/colander (if you don't) face-up over the saucepan (not in the water, but resting on it like a lid). Cover and allow the food to cook. The boiling water below it will release steam, which will be trapped in the basket and which is what will cook your food. And that's it, guys and gals – steamed!

NB: you can also buy purpose-made steamers that are quicker and even easier to use.

BAKING

Basically, baking is the process of cooking food in the oven with dry heat. ... The food can be flavoured but is not soaked in any oil or fat. And since you are now fully versed in the workings of the oven, all I need say is put the food in the pre-heated oven, wait, take it out, and it is baked.

NB: depending on what you are baking, you might find that the food has a tendency to stick to the pan. To avoid this, grease the pan with a thin coating of oil or margarine, or line it with greaseproof, oven-safe paper.

ROASTING

This process is exactly the same thing as baking, except that the food is cooked in oil or fat.

GRILLING

Unlike baking or roasting, which cooks food by heating up the whole oven, grilling is a method of cooking food by direct dry heat, the same way that you cook on a barbeque. This means that the food needs to be placed directly beneath the grill (usually located at the top of the oven, or you might have a separate grill altogether), and the grill must be hot before you start (so pre-heat the oven if your grill is there).

Once this is done, the food should be placed directly onto the grill pan or in an oven tray to catch the drips as the food cooks. If the food is particularly messy, you can place a sheet of foil on the tray before adding the food, but bear in mind that this will hinder the concept of direct heat in the grilling process. Anyway, you are now grilling! Wait until cooked and remove.

The only caution here is to check that the food is completely cooked on the inside (even if it looks burnt on the outside), as grilling, which creates a tasty crispy layer on the edge of food, can sometimes hide a raw centre. You might not run a restaurant, and dinner guests might not sue if poisoned, but they're unlikely to be happy after sitting in casualty for four hours, and you run the risk of losing all of your friends, as well as your own stomach.

Getting fancy

For those of you who have sailed through the basics, there are, of course, hundreds of cooking terms reserved for the more advanced, and for the fancy cookbooks. This, however, is not a fancy cookbook. Nevertheless, here's a

very brief description of some of the most commonly used
– and misunderstood – parts of culinary terminology:

- **Basting:** pouring dripping, fat or stock over food
  while cooking.
- **Blanching:** very briefly submerging foods in boiling
  water either to cook them partially or to remove skin
  and/or bitterness.
- **Braising:** a method of cooking whereby food is first
  browned in fat, then tightly covered and cooked in a
  small amount of liquid at a low heat for a lengthy
  period of time.
- **Browning:** cooking food very quickly over a high
  heat, so that the surface turns brown while the interi-
  or stays moist. Usually done on the hob.
- **Brushing:** using a pastry or basting brush to add
  liquid (such as melted butter) to the surface of food.
- **Dicing:** cutting into small cubes.
- **Dusting:** sprinkling food, usually with sugar or flour.
- **Folding:** a technique used to combine gently a light,
  airy mixture with a heavier mixture. The lighter
  mixture is placed on top of the heavier one in a large
  bowl and they are then literally folded together,
  using a rubber spatula (or a metal spoon for eggs),
  with a down-up-across-up-and-over motion.
- **Garnishing:** decorating food, usually with herbs.
- **Kneading:** a technique used to mix and work dough
  to form a pliable lump.

- **Marinating:** letting food stand in a mixture called a marinade (such as a liquid, dry-rub, or paste) before cooking, to tenderise and/or add flavour.
- **Parboiling:** to boil food partially, for a short period of time, before cooking by another method.
- **Sautéeing:** frying in a very small amount of oil.
- **Seasoning:** basically, adding stuff like salt, pepper, and so on, to the food.
- **Sieving:** straining liquid or food through a sieve.
- **Straining:** see sieving, but the holes in a strainer are larger.
- **Stir-frying:** quickly frying small pieces of food in a large pan (preferably a wok) over very high heat while constantly stirring the food. Very little oil or fat is used.
- **Tossing:** mixing with a rising-and-falling action.
- **Trussing:** binding poultry for roasting using string or skewers.
- **Whisking:** beating food with a whisk until well mixed.

Food preparation – kill or be killed

When it comes to food preparation, don't expect pages about beautiful displays or methods of marinating, basting or parboiling. I'm dealing only with the basics, the real core of food survival, and there's only one real issue to deal with here: germs.

Germs are everywhere when it comes to food, but they needn't be an issue so long as you remember the three Ws: wash, wash and wash. However, there's no need to go over the top, put that soap down, we don't need to marinate our potatoes in detergent! All I'm saying is: make sure you rinse food that comes out of the ground, and make sure you wash your hands after touching food that comes from an animal. After all, you wouldn't want a surgeon to perform a heart transplant and then move straight on to preparing the salad, would you?

Meat, poultry and fish can all carry some nasty bacteria that can make you seriously ill. Cooking it properly gets rid of these germs, so they don't need to be washed themselves, but since you don't generally leave your hands in the oven to cook, they must be washed thoroughly before you touch anything else. That means DON'T just move the fruit bowl out of the way to find a space for the marinating meat, DON'T wipe your hands on the tea towel you're later going to use to dry the crockery with, and DON'T open the cupboard to get a glass of water. Don't do any of these things until you've washed your hands thoroughly, as the bacteria will live on everything you've touched, cunningly waiting to strike. For this reason, it's also important to wash any surface that the meat has touched, properly, BEFORE it touches anything else. Yes, I know this means you may have to clean up twice, but trust me, an extra couple of minutes in the kitchen is far better than weeks hunched over a toilet seat.

Fruit and veg is a different story. The germs on them are not normally so potent, and if you cut out any bruising (where bacteria thrives), you've probably got most of it. However, these foods do come out of the ground or off trees, they have been submerged in dirt, a lot of them are covered in pesticides, and you never know what animal has been nosing around it, or worse. So, it's a good idea to wash it under a cold tap to get rid of any lingering dirt. Soap is not necessary, and in fact is probably more dangerous for you if ingested than the dirt was in the first place.

What to cook

Are you seriously expecting me to tell you what you should be cooking? How the heck do I know? I've no idea if you're a vegetarian, a carnivore or if you're allergic to nuts. I have no qualifications in the field of nutrition. And I don't have a clue if you've got a sweet tooth, a pasta addiction or a strange obsession with lettuce. However, what I can give you is a basic run-down of what some of the main food groups are and what they do, with a quick precursor that balance is usually best. If you were listening in food technology at school, then you already know all this. But since that was when you were 13, and you were probably passing notes instead of listening to the ever-so passionate teacher, there's a high chance that you don't:

- **Calcium:** found in dairy products, green vegetables, nuts, seeds and soya products. Helps strengthen our bones and gives you that Hollywood smile.
- **Carbohydrates:** found in complex (healthy) form in rice, bread, cereal, fruits, legumes (peas, beans and lentils) and vegetables, and in simple (less healthy) form in foods containing refined sugar. They are our most readily used source of energy – which is why athletes 'carb up' before a race – and in the healthy form also contain a lot of nutrients.
- **Fat:** hold on, don't look away with a huff and exclaim, 'Fat! I don't want fat!' Some fat is good for you and in fact is an essential nutrient. 'Good' (poly and unsaturated) fats can be found in olive and sunflower oils, nuts, seeds, oily fish and soya foods. They are a great energy source and actually help to reduce cholesterol. 'Bad' (saturated) fats, however, raise cholesterol, increasing your risk of heart disease. They are found in meat, cheese, butter, biscuits, cakes ... and most things that taste good. A bit of these are OK, but try not to overload.
- **Fibre:** found in cereals, rice, pasta, fruit, legumes, lentils, vegetables and wholegrain breads. Many people believe that fibre is important in preventing cancer as well as heart disease because it lowers cholesterol and controls blood sugar. It's also important to ensure regular trips to the loo.
- **Iron:** found in cereals, green leafy vegetables, nuts,

seeds, meat, wholegrain breads and legumes. It's important for healthy blood.

- **Potassium:** found in fruit, veg, meat, milk and grains. It's important for nerve function to the muscles, and therefore the heart.
- **Protein:** found in meat, fish, cheese, eggs, nuts, soya, baked beans and whole grains. It's essential for the growth of body cells, maintaining and replacing the tissues in your body, for making antibodies that fight infection, and for making haemoglobin, which carries oxygen around your body.
- **Sodium:** found in salt. It helps regulate blood pressure and water balance, and works with potassium to control blood acidity. However, too much salt can lead to high blood pressure, which could in turn lead to a stroke.

NB: calories are simply a measurement of energy. It's better to watch what kind of food you're eating (that is, fat, fibre, carbohydrate, and so on) and keep a healthy balance, rather than simply counting the calories on the back of chocolate bars. After all, five chocolate bars and a Coke isn't a healthy day's diet, even if you haven't eaten loads of calories.

Storage – save it for later

So, you've successfully balanced your nutrients, mastered your equipment, managed to become so fluent in the language of cuisine that the local baker thinks you're French, and successfully hosted a dinner party without giving any of your guests salmonella. You should now have an array of delicious leftovers – perfect for ensuring that after such an exhausting evening's hosting you don't have to touch the hob again for a whole week. And, if you're really efficient, you may even have been shopping to restock on all the staple items that are lining the stomachs of you and your full friends. We now enter the next phase of food survival: storage.

Food generally comes in three types. No, I'm not talking meat, fruit and veg, nor am I ranting about killer carbs, friendly fats, or those acceptable on the berry diet. My distinction is far more sweeping and much more philosophic ... where does it belong?

PANTRY

(For those of you who don't live in mansions, or in the 19th century, by pantry I really mean cupboard or any place that is clean, cool and dry. But doesn't pantry sound fancier!)

Foods safe for the pantry include most canned goods, cereal, pasta, dry mixes, crisps, tea, coffee and various bottled sauces. Basically, anything that doesn't tell you to freeze or refrigerate.

Most of these goods have a long shelf (or health) life. This means that they can be kept for a long period of time (sometimes years) before they go off. However, always make sure you check the label, as, since most people aren't obsessive enough to rotate their goods as they buy new ones, an innocent can of tuna can loiter at the back of a cupboard for a decade before it's tragically let loose in your stomach. Also, never eat anything that is leaking, badly dented, cracked, or that smells, even if the shelf life hasn't passed.

....

NB: don't store food in cabinets over ovens, hobs, radiators or fridge exhausts, as extremes of hot and cold can wreak havoc on these goods, and completely invalidate the shelf lives that you are so painstakingly and triumphantly taking the time to read.

....

REFRIGERATOR

Perhaps the greatest liberating force known to man, the refrigerator has unleashed us all from the shackles of daily shopping and allowed us to be grocery-lazy for at least six days a week. Can you even imagine a time when you had to fetch fresh food every day? Well, it wasn't all that long ago ... all hail the refrigerator!

The fridge allows us to preserve the freshness of food

and slow down the growth of bacteria so that food stays edible for a much longer period of time, especially if everything is stored in airtight containers. However, fridge food will still go off, so make sure to check it out before you gulp it in.

The fridge should be kept at a temperature of 4.5°C/40°F or below, and must not be overloaded, as this can stop the air circulating and mean that some dark corners, where only the bravest of lettuces lurk, aren't being kept cold.

Most foods come in containers suited to refrigeration, but make sure that meat and poultry are completely sealed so that they don't spread their bacteria around. Putting them in plastic bags is always a good way to double-up on prevention, and it's best to put them in the coldest part of the fridge. However, be careful that the fridge is not too cold, otherwise you might find your meat frozen.

....

NB: when storing cooked items, let them cool down before putting them in the fridge, otherwise there's a danger that they might warm everything else up.

....

FREEZER

Well, if the fridge allowed us not to shop for a week, the freezer means we need hardly buy anything for a month. With the help of the handy freezer, we can simply stock up on an array of ready-made meals and defrost a different delight in the microwave each night ... all hail the freezer!

There's not much that can go wrong in the way of storage at this point: put the food in the freezer. However, do make sure that everything is packed and sealed properly, and try to use it within a couple of months to prevent 'freezer burn'. Alternatively, if you know you're going to store it for longer, double wrap it in a plastic bag, as store packaging is sometimes not quite airtight.

Defrosting is where things become a tiny bit trickier, because it means that you might need to think ahead. Food must be thawed in one of three places only: in the refrigerator, under cold running water, or in the microwave. And, unless thawed in the fridge, once completely defrosted, it must be cooked immediately.

If you have a microwave, you have no problem, as this is a relatively quick process and the instructions on the pack will usually tell you how long to defrost it for. However, the other two methods take time, so, especially if you're planning to defrost in the fridge, make sure you take the food out of the freezer the night before, or at the very latest, that morning, although some foods can take days to defrost in this way, if they're large. Also, remember to place a tray underneath whatever you are defrosting to catch any juices that may thaw and drip. If defrosting under cold running water, make sure you first place the food in a sealed plastic bag to prevent the bacteria from running off and contaminating the rest of your kitchen. This is especially important in the case of shellfish and poultry, which can contain high levels of potent bacteria.

....

NB: meat, poultry and fish should NEVER be thawed on the kitchen counter, in a cold room, or outside, as these methods encourage the growth of the bacteria that has been frozen for months and is just waiting to get its greedy little paws on your stomach. (Although it's usually OK to thaw baked goods on the counter.)

....

THE MOULDY CHEESE QUESTION

After years of buying too much food to eat before it all goes off, or, especially at uni, finding myself penniless and unable to buy new food, I have adopted the somewhat controversial policy of: if you can't see the mould, it's not too old. For instance, if one slice of bread is showing visible mould, that doesn't necessarily mean the whole loaf has gone off. And if a tub of cream cheese or jam is sprouting a small tuft of fuzz, it can be tempting to simply scoop it out and use a fuzz-free bit.

However, NEVER take the chance on meat, fish or poultry – and bear in mind that eating old food is itself an extreme sport ... entirely at your own risk.

Cleaning up – the aftermath

Having made your wonderful meal and even put away all your leftovers, you may now be standing around the kitchen wondering what it is that doesn't quite seem right. Here's a hint: the saucepan is caked in burnt sauce, the worktops are covered in crumbs and splashed salad dressing, and there's a stack of plates next to the sink that could rival the leaning tower of Pisa. The solution: you need to clean up.

Yes, I know it's boring, you're tired, feel like an over-fed cat, and just want to crash out in front of the TV, but no, it can't wait until the morning. And if you do it quickly – or rope your dinner guests into helping before they leave – it really won't take that long.

The first task is to put everything that can go into the dishwasher, in the dishwasher. (If you don't have a dishwasher, then sorry, the process is going to take quite a bit longer and you're going to get prune-hands and a wet top.) Dishwasher items include crockery, cutlery, glasses, most serving bowls and some saucepans. It doesn't include anything made of brushed metal, some delicate glass, bone- or wooden-handled cutlery (although wooden spoons and cooking utensils are OK), or anything you're going to be devastated about if left with a watermark. It also doesn't include anything that is still caked with food. Everything must be rinsed before it goes into the dishwasher, otherwise you're going to get little particles of food wedged into the crevices of all your kitchenware and you'll wonder whether anything has been cleaned at all. On the other hand, if you prefer the patterned look, sprinkles of ground-in broccoli will certainly liven up your white plate set.

Anything that won't come clean with a quick rinse needs to be hand washed, and possibly soaked. This involves leaving it in hot water and washing-up liquid for a while ('a while' varies depending on just how ground-in the dirt is: anything from a few minutes to overnight), and then washing with a dishcloth, scrubbing brush or scourer to get it really clean. Less stained items can be cleaned straight away with washing-up liquid and hot water, but remember to rinse everything afterwards to make sure no chemicals remain.

You should now have a steaming stack of sparkling glasses and saucepans, which you can either leave to drip-dry (preferably on a draining board, or over a tea towel) or take the time to dry and put away – it depends on how obsessive/tired you are. Next – and finally – you have to clean your worktops. Wet a dishcloth with hot water, spray on some disinfectant, and wipe down those sides. To reach true grown-up status, it is necessary to catch all those icky slivers of food in your hand, instead of brushing them onto the floor where they will: a) get trodden in, stick to your shoe and spread their germs everywhere you walk; b) force you to clean the floor; or c) get eaten by the dog/cat/baby who will then develop food poisoning, throw up and create a lot more cleaning up for you in the long run. Once this is done, wash the cloth, rinse out the sink, wash your hands, and you're done!

At this point, you will be either feeling a huge sense of satisfaction, smug in the knowledge that there is no kitchen task too great for you; or, you will be rueing the day you ever moved out of home. If the latter is the case, never fear. Practice really does make perfect and if at first you don't succeed, try, try and try again. If, however, you do try again, and again, and again, and still fail to muster up any kind of meal, don't worry, there remain some very valid options: a) get a kitchen-friendly girlfriend/boyfriend, b) earn lots and lots of money so that you can employ a personal chef, or c) move back in with your mum.

2
HEALTH: STAYING ALIVE

Having mastered the art of food survival, you should now be able to keep yourself alive for a sustained period of time. But what happens if you get ill? When you're a kid and you're ill, everyone makes a fuss – or, at least, your parents do. They confine you to bed (or, if you're really lucky, to a duvet on the couch in front of the TV), they bring you juice (to bulk up on vitamin C), water (to flush out the bug), hot milk and butter (for your throat), toast and honey (to settle your stomach), and chicken noodle soup (Jewish penicillin and a cure for everything.) But when you're grown up, suddenly nobody seems to care. Nobody brings you tissues, or calls your work for you to tell them you're sick. Nobody takes your temperature or runs out to buy you Lemsip. And nobody forces you to go and see the doctor, even when you feel like you're at death's door. You see, for some reason, you're expected to be responsible and mature enough to do these things yourself. But the thing is, when you're ill, you don't want to be responsible – all you want is some chicken noodle soup and your mum.

Even worse than being ill yourself, however, is when you're in a relationship, or living with a friend, and they get sick. Suddenly you're the one who's supposed to act mature and know exactly what to do. Of course, you remember some of the home remedies practised on you as a child, but the old 'feed a cold, starve a fever' adage doesn't apply to stomach bugs, and tonsillitis can't be cured by hot milk. Being in charge is a lot of pressure and it's hard to know what to do.

So, how do you know when to go to casualty, when to go to the doctor, or when to just tuck yourself up in bed? When you're ill, the last thing you want to do is to think for yourself. So don't. I've done the thinking for you.

Levels of illness

When you go to the doctor, it's difficult not to notice all the people coughing and sneezing next to you; after all, you're likely to be waiting with them for some time. And while part of you feels that being cooped up with them will make you contract something far worse than whatever brought you to the doctor in the first place, when you look around you, some of them don't look ill at all. In fact, some of them look like they're faking, or have nothing that a bit of cough mixture couldn't sort out, whereas you really need to see a doctor. Once you've decided that, and then watched them get seen before you, it's a slippery slope towards rage and resentment.

But the thing is, you're probably right. Lots of people go to the doctor when they don't need to, or casualty when a doctor would do, which adds unnecessary pressure to already stretched facilities. So, while you should obviously seek help when you need to, try to pick the service that's right for your level of illness.

If you're not sure *which* service is right, or if you think you need *some* medical advice, but it's the middle of the night and not quite up to casualty level, the NHS has set up a helpline called NHS Direct. This line is open all day, every day and is run by nurses who'll either give you advice themselves, or call you back after speaking to a doctor. They'll then advise you how to treat the problem, or tell you to seek further help. Of course, in most cases you'll probably be able to work out for yourself what level of help you need, but if you're struggling, here are a few pointers:

PHARMACY

Pharmacists are medicine experts – like modern-day witch doctors – so they can give you in-depth advice about what potion you should be taking. Often, they'll even be able to give you over the counter what you've waited an hour in the doctor's for them to recommend. Consequently, they're the perfect people to talk to if you're suffering from minor ailments: a cold or flu, a cough or sore throat, a minor rash or a migraine, and so on. (They are not the people to speak to if you have a gushing head wound.) If it's beyond their expertise, they'll tell you to see a doctor, but they're a great first stop.

NB: it's a good idea always to keep a small-scale pharmacy in your own home; for example, plasters, paracetemol, antiseptic cream, cough syrup. (Making it all the way to the pharmacy when you're coughing at every step can feel akin to climbing Everest on a windy day.)

NHS WALK-IN CENTRES

If you're a commuter, GP opening times and appointment -booking systems are probably a major bugbear.

Commuters often leave for work before their GP surgery has opened, get home after it's shut, and at some practices you can't even book an appointment in advance so that you can arrange time off work. Not particularly helpful. Of course, some annoying GP receptionists will huffily argue that if you're ill enough to see a GP then you shouldn't be at work anyway, but that's simply not true. You might have an exotic rash that doesn't make you feel ill but is slowly turning you into a lizard. Or, you might have a swollen ankle that doesn't stop you typing into a computer but isn't exactly a picture of health.

Never fear. There are now over 50 NHS walk-in centres across the UK where you can drop in without an appointment and be treated for common ailments without charge. They're open from early morning to late evening, seven days a week, and some are conveniently located near main train stations. The only drawback is that while the experienced nurses who run them can advise you about most non-urgent conditions, you'll still need to speak to a doctor for more serious problems.

....

NB: if you get ill at work, you can make an emergency appointment with a local GP in that area. Often companies will even offer schemes that provide for this – commuters take note.

....

DOCTOR

You need to see a doctor when minor ailments (a cough, sore throat, and so on) persist despite over-the-counter medication, or when you have problems that need more expertise. It can be difficult to know when ailments are serious enough to warrant a doctor (for example, meningitis can often be mistaken in its early stages for a cold). So, despite having warned against unnecessary GP visits, if you're worried about a problem, or can't place the symptoms, it's better to be safe than sorry. To make an appointment, follow the booking procedures of your particular surgery.

Alternatively, if you're so ill that you can't even make it to the surgery, GPs may visit you at home ... if you pass their test of being sick enough. If your surgery offers this, the decision is meant to be made by the doctor or nurse, but often power-tripping receptionists will ask you a range of aggressive questions that make you feel like you're faking and shouldn't be taking up the doctor's time. Stick to your guns. When ill, the last thing you want is an argument, but be firm, after all, your taxes pay for this service.

If you need to see a doctor when the surgery's closed, there will usually be an emergency contact number on its answering machine. Alternatively, call NHS Direct, who may advise you go to casualty if the problem can't wait.

....

NB: when ill, some people immediately make a dash for the doctor and automatically ask for antibiotics. Antibiotics are a bit of a miracle drug, but they cure only

bacterial infections, not viral infections. And since all colds, for example, are caused by viruses, antibiotics won't help – better to stick with the pharmacy.

....

CASUALTY

Accident and Emergency (A&E) departments are not synonymous with an out-of-hours GP. They are set up to deal with *serious emergency* illness or injury, not your runny nose. However, not all emergencies are easy to spot. Obviously, if someone's unconscious – that's an emergency. It's also an emergency if: they stop breathing; lose a lot of blood; break a bone; have a heart attack; are severely burned; and so on. But what if you've got a really aggressive case of puking? Or what if you have a cut that may or may not need stitches? If you're not sure, call NHS Direct.

....

NB: you can often get less serious injuries that still need emergency attention treated at minor injury units. These are run by experienced nurse practitioners (I know they're not doctors, but haven't you ever watched *ER*? Some nurses really know their stuff!), and you should get seen much faster than in A&E where more serious complaints will be dealt with first. These units are good for injuries such as sprains, fractures, bites, cuts and infected wounds. (Ask your local health authority where the nearest unit is.)

....

AMBULANCE (DIAL 999)

Arriving at A&E in an ambulance may be dramatic but it doesn't get you seen first – patients are still seen in order of need. And since sometimes you can get to casualty faster than an ambulance will be able to, especially if you live close to a hospital, it might be better just to go there yourself. (This doesn't mean, however, that you can speed through traffic and stick your head out the car window making siren noises.) You should also make your own way there if the problem isn't time-critical – for example, a broken arm won't be any more broken if it's seen five minutes later.

However, for anything that is time-critical, or could be worsened by your moving the injured person (for example, back or neck injuries), it's better to leave it to the ambulance services who can move them professionally and start treating them straight away. You should *always* call an ambulance if the person has severe chest pain or difficulty breathing.

The doctor – in depth

So, you've done the pharmacy thing, you don't need casualty, let's face it – for most levels of illness your first port of call will be the bog-standard doctor. The first task on the road to health, therefore, is finding a GP surgery. For many people who've grown up with a family doctor who remembers every cut and bruise they've had since the age of nought, finding a new surgery can be an unwanted change. In fact, I have a friend who lives in London but still travels three hours to see her old doctor in Manchester – she shall remain anonymous since it's actually against the rules of the NHS to remain with a surgery once you have left its catchment area.

Chances are that you will already have noticed a local surgery in your area. However, if you haven't, you can find out where your nearest one is either by calling your local Primary Care Trust (PCT), or by doing a local search on the NHS Direct website.

NB: you can find your local Primary Care Trust by looking in the Yellow Pages, on the Internet, or by calling one of the phone directory services.

You'll generally have a choice of at least two or three surgeries in whose catchment area you live. However, they might not all be accepting new patients. Start by choosing a surgery, then call it up and ask to register. If they're full, you may be refused (although they must give you a written reason explaining this), and you should then move on to the next surgery that is nearest to you.

However, in most cases the surgery should be able to accept you and will begin by sending you some registration forms or asking you to go into the surgery to fill them in. When you register, you'll be asked for your

NHS medical card. I notice a flash of consternation wrinkling your brow. Have you never heard of a medical card? Basically, it contains your NHS number, personal details such as your name, address and date of birth, and should be in your possession. If, however, you don't have one (or have somehow 'misplaced' it), the receptionist will give you a form to fill in. When this has been completed and returned, your local PCT will transfer your medical records to your new surgery and your new medical card should arrive at your home address.

Once registered, you'll be given details of the surgery, including opening times, clinics and appointment procedures. You may also be asked to come in to be given a new patient check to assess your general health. As well as performing a number of routine tests (for example, blood pressure, weight, and, sorry boys, it's time to cough ...), the doctor will ask you about past medical problems, on-going medical problems, medicines you take, allergies and the contact details of your previous doctor, so make sure you have this information with you.

You will then become a fully-fledged member of the surgery, entitled to nag the receptionists and be a complete nuisance every time you feel ill. If, however, you get ill while away from home, don't worry, you don't have to drive all the way back to see your own GP. You can receive emergency treatment at any NHS surgery for up to 14 days without being registered, and you can also register as a temporary patient if you're going to be away from home for an extended length of time.

A NOTE ON PRESCRIPTIONS

For some reason, coming out of the doctor with a prescription in hand feels like a victory. It is proof positive that you really are ill, you really do deserve sympathy, and your illness has an actual name. Without one, you will either be forever known as a faker, or be left endlessly searching for a more satisfying description of your illness than simply, 'it's a low grade virus', which roughly translates as: 'we don't have a clue.'

If you're given a prescription, you'll need to take it to a pharmacy to be dispensed. (Simply fill in and sign the back of the form, then give it to the pharmacist.) However, be prepared that usually you will have to pay for your prescription, unless you're eligible for free or reduced costs.

SICK NOTES

Having obtained your diagnosis and your prescription, the next thing to do is secure the day off work. To do this, simply phone the office, squeeze the end of your nose to provide the obligatory nasality, and let whoever's in charge know that you won't be there because you're ill. Usually, they'll accept this and wish you better. However, if you're unfortunate enough to have a boss that demands blood, stand firm. You are legally entitled to time off when ill, and you don't need your parents or guardian to write a note to prove it.

However, some companies will actually require a sick note. Not from your parents, but from your doctor. (When you need one should be specified in your contract, but it's usually required after you have been away ill for about a week.) To get a sick note, simply make an appointment with your GP, but be prepared that, in some cases, you'll have to pay for the certificate they give you.

When you return to work – still sniffing for authenticity – you'll be asked to fill out a self-certification form which asks you how long you were off sick and, most critically, why. (I know, you don't really want your boss knowing that you had severe menstrual cramps or diarrhoea, but, sorry, it can't be avoided.)

....

NB: if you were faking it, make up some vague symptoms and try to avoid the old returning-to-work-after-being-'sick' trick with an obvious tan.

....

Specialist advice

While the bog-standard GP covers a range of sins, there are some problems that they simply can't help you with, but they may know a man who can. You need to see a specialist when your problem goes beyond the expertise of your GP, or when the ailment doesn't improve after extensive GP treatment. It may be your doctor who suggests it, or it may be you who asks, but either way, you need him to write you a letter of referral first (in most cases, this applies even if you see the specialist privately). To get a referral, simply make an appointment with your GP and ask away.

NB: your GP will usually recommend a particular person to treat you, but if you have private insurance, you can ask them or your GP for a list of specialists, or request a particular one.

Dentist

The best time to join a dentist is *before* you get a toothache – if you ever get one, you'll understand why. Toothache can be VERY painful, and very costly too, so nip it in the bud ASAP.

To find and register with a dentist, search in exactly the same way as you did with your GP. The treatment can then be carried out entirely under the NHS (although NHS practices are now more and more difficult to find), privately, or through a mixture of both, although you have to specify which when you join the surgery. This, however, isn't set in stone, as you may find that you later want to change your mind depending on your level of vanity. For example, the NHS will give you a filling in a back tooth, but if you want that filling to be white, you will have to cough up the cash for private treatment. Private dental care is often covered under health insurance policies, so check what you are covered for before you start to pay for anything yourself. And if you're entitled to any free or reduced-cost treatment under the NHS, remember to tell your dentist before the treatment is carried out. If you don't remember, don't worry – it's not too late. Just ask the dental receptionist for a refund claim form.

Depending on the perfection of your smile, you will need to see the dentist at different intervals, but at least every 15 months. (Your registration will expire if you fail do this.)

If you need emergency treatment, most dental practices will have an answering machine message instructing you what to do, just like the GP. If they don't, contact NHS Direct for advice. And if you need urgent care but still haven't got yourself registered with a practice, you can always go to one of the new NHS Dental Access Centres. (You may also want to invest in a To Do list and put 'Join a dentist' at the top.) Appointments are not always necessary, normal NHS charges apply, and you can receive the same treatment as you would at normal surgeries. However, urgent cases will be prioritised so you may be waiting a while.

NB: once you get past the age of around 21, a normal dentist is not enough to keep on top of your oral hygiene – you will need to see a hygienist as well. Unfortunately, this is not the most pleasant of experiences as they tend to poke around a lot more than dentists do, but your mouth will thank you long-term. Ordinarily, your dentist will put you in touch with a hygienist automatically, but if they don't, ask them to recommend one for you.

Optician

You may think that you have 20:20 vision, your eyes are perfect, and you have absolutely no need for an optician. Think again. Opticians recommend that everyone has an eye test at least every two years, because they test not only your vision, but also the condition of your eye. The state of your inner and outer eye can reveal health problems (such as diabetes and glaucoma) far earlier than if you wait for other symptoms to arise, so it's important to have regular checks.

In fact, eye tests are considered so important, that they are provided free on the NHS, although only for certain people. To find out if you qualify, call NHS Direct or your local health authority. You may also be provided with a voucher to help towards the cost of glasses.

To find an optician, search in the same way as you did for doctors and dentists, or simply walk down the high street until you find one. There are, however, three types of opticians, and you should be aware which type you are going to, as not all of them will conduct as thorough an examination as others:

- **Optometrists:** aka ophthalmic opticians, these are the dons of opticians – the most specialised. They check your vision, look for signs of disease, and prescribe and fit glasses and contact lenses. They may also recommend you see a doctor or an eye surgeon.
- **Ophthalmic medical practitioners:** these are medical doctors who are also trained to carry out eye exams and prescribe glasses.
- **Dispensing opticians:** these fit and sell glasses, but they're not trained to give eye tests. They can, however, give you advice about types of lenses and frames.

Having chosen your optician, you'll start off with an eye test. Eye tests are not supposed to make you feel stupid; there is no wrong answer! However, there's something about doing a test – any kind of test – that puts you on edge and makes you feel a bit dumb. I mean, after the optician has asked you which side looks clearer for the seventh time, it's no wonder that you're beginning to have trouble. Don't panic. Just be as honest as you can and try not to hit the optician when they ask you the same question for the eighth time.

The optician will let you know what you need to do from here. You may need glasses, further tests or medication, or you may simply need to come back in two years.

Family planning

Both men and women can obtain free, confidential advice about contraception and sexual health at a Family Planning Clinic (FPC), which is able to run tests for sexually transmitted infections (STIs), prescribe the pill, conduct cervical screening, give pregnancy tests, fit caps and coils, offer counselling and carry out progesterone injections for patients during infertility treatment. They will also usually give you a free goody bag full of contraceptives if you want one.

Many of these services are, of course, also available at a doctor's surgery. However, FPCs are specifically set up to deal with sex-related issues – and you may feel more comfortable discussing them anonymously with a person who has these issues coming out of their ears rather than with the friendly old doctor who still remembers when you were in nappies.

FPCs deal with men and women of all ages, and you can go by yourself, with a friend, or with a partner, and without them informing anyone of your visit. You may need to book an appointment, but most FPCs also have walk-in clinics.

Other specialists and alternative therapy

There are long lists of other specialists that we just don't have room for here, but even if you visited every one of them, traditional medicine doesn't always cure everything. Consequently, many people look to alternative treatments for help. Before you ask, no, I'm not only talking about Madonna, Gwyneth Paltrow and the crazy monkey in *The Lion King*. Many alternative therapies are now very mainstream and some are even covered by the NHS upon GP referral. However, these specialists can also be seen privately and without referral. Search for them in the same way as the previous specialists, or through personal recommendation. Just make sure that the specialist has the appropriate qualifications. Below is a list of who does what:

ACUPUNCTURE

One of the oldest medical techniques in the world, acupuncture is used to relieve all sorts of pain, particularly back pain, and involves the insertion of thin needles in various anatomical points on the body. (Yes, you will end up lying on a table and looking like a hedgehog, with long needles coming out of your little toe.) Although acupuncture is an 'alternative' therapy it's widely respected by many people all over the world and may even be recommended by your GP.

ALEXANDER TECHNIQUE

Rather than a quick-fix solution, this is a long-term technique of correcting posture and everyday habits of movement to release tension and improve co-ordination. It is particularly good for bad backs.

AROMATHERAPY

This is a holistic therapy that aims to prevent and cure injury and illness. It's based on the skilled use of essential oils, often administered through massage, focusing on the mind, body and spirit.

CHIROPODY/PODIATRY

There is no difference between chiropody and podiatry – the two terms can be used interchangeably. Both deal with the foot and lower limb, with typical treatment involving corns, verrucas, athlete's foot, in-growing toenails and bunions. Chiropodists and podiatrists can also analyse the way you stand, walk and run, prescribing orthotics (specially designed insoles that are worn inside the shoe to control abnormal foot function and/or control painful areas of the foot) if need be.

CHIROPRACTIC

A form of spinal manipulation, chiropractic is one of the oldest healing practices. It's particularly used to treat back and neck pain, but stems from the theory that the whole body has a natural healing ability controlled by the nervous system that has its source in the spinal column. Many chiropractors believe that this 'flow' is interrupted when vertebrae are misaligned, so they try to manipulate the spine so that the flow is clear.

HOMEOPATHY

An alternative therapy that aims to stimulate the body's defence mechanisms to treat or prevent illness, homeo-pathy involves the prescription of tailored remedies that take in the patient's entire lifestyle, mental and physical state. The remedies are based on the concept of giving very small doses of substances that, if given to a healthy person, would produce symptoms similar to those being suffered by the patient. (Sounds weird, but there is actually a similar logic around allergy treatment and vaccines.)

MASSAGE

This involves a variety of techniques aiming to alleviate stress, tension, and minor injury in the body's soft tissues (muscles, tendons and ligaments). It works through manipulation, pressure and movement. Great for sore muscles, and relaxing even if you're not sore.

NUTRITION

Often suggested as a supplement to other treatment, nutrition involves examining individual food intake patterns. Recommendations are then made to modify eating habits with the aim of improving general health or a particular problem. It may also include analysis of general lifestyle, exercise, and so on.

OSTEOPATHY

The focus for osteopaths is the musculo-skeletal system (bones, joints, muscles, ligaments and tissue). They usually treat injuries, but also problems caused by disease, in a similar way to physiotherapists. However, they differ in that they use only manual techniques without the use of mechanical equipment.

PHYSIOTHERAPY

This is also known as physical therapy, and is the treatment of disease or injury by physical therapeutic means (as opposed to surgery and medicine). Generally, it includes massage, manipulation and patient education, as well as ultrasound and other mechanical methods. Particularly good for musculo-skeletal issues, especially back pain, but also a whole range of problems, including asthma, heart disease and osteoarthritis.

PILATES, YOGA, AND SO ON

There are a number of therapeutic body-conditioning programmes that have become popular for treating specific problems, as well as promoting general fitness and well-being, particularly among those who enjoy turning their bodies into a human pretzel. Two of the most common are yoga and Pilates – classes for which can be found at most fitness centres. Yoga dates back many thousands of years (yes, before Madonna) and focuses on stretching postures, breathing and meditation techniques to tone the body and calm the mind. Pilates also incorporates body and mind, but focuses mainly on breathing and core strength and stability. It is known to be particularly good for bad backs.

REFLEXOLOGY

This is a holistic therapy in which pressure is applied to the feet and hands. The theory behind it is that all of the body's internal structures are mirrored in miniature 'reflex zones' in the feet and hands, so, by manipulating these reflexes, the whole body can be treated.

Looking after yourself – special issues

As you can see, specialists exist to treat almost anything. Nevertheless, there are times when, if you can avoid it, you'd simply rather not ask. So, for the doctor-shy, here are a few handy pointers:

CONTRACEPTION

There exists a whole chocolate box of contraception – the key is knowing exactly which one you're gonna get. They're all different, with varying success rates, and some need medical prescription whereas others can be found at the local petrol station. It's all a matter of personal choice, so give them a try and see which is best for you:

Most safe

- Sterilisation (tubal litigation or vasectomy)
- Implant
- Injectable contraception
- Combined contraceptive pill
- Progestogen-only pill
- Intra-uterine device (IUD)
- Intra-uterine system (IUS)
- Condom (condoms are the only form of contraception that protect against disease)
- Female condom
- Diaphragm
- Ovulation predictor

Less safe

- Withdrawal
- Rhythm method

....

NB: there now exists a male contraceptive pill designed to block sperm production. (Yep, pretty soon men will be lucky enough to take some weird drug that sends their hormones into chaos too!) But breathe, boys – it's not yet available in the UK.

....

The morning-after scare

There are two types of emergency contraception that can be used *after* having sex if you think you might be pregnant. They do NOT give protection against disease.

Morning-after pill: these are available on prescription from your doctor, the Family Planning Clinic, or over the counter at the pharmacy. However, these pills contain strong stuff, so while they're a saviour in an emergency, they should not be thought of as simply another form of contraception.

IUD: this can be fitted by a doctor or nurse, as soon as possible after having sex, but usually within five days. It works by making it difficult for the sperm to get through to the egg, and for the egg to implant in the womb.

HANGOVERS

Ah, the interminable 'it must have been food poisoning' sickness. The illness where you can't tell your boss why you're bleary-eyed, or explain to your lecturer why you have to run to the toilet halfway through the very interesting debate; because it is entirely self-induced and no sympathy is warranted (except, perhaps from your similarly hungover friends). So, how do you cure it? Well, first we must understand it – we must get inside its head:

What is a hangover?

OK clever-clogs, we all know that a hangover is what you get when you've had too much to drink, but, more scientifically, a hangover is a combination of dehydration and intoxication. Alcohol itself is a mild depressant drug, and you are suffering from an overdose. Plus, by flushing so many important nutrients out of your body, you are also in metabolic shock. The symptoms therefore include nausea, a headache, fatigue, the jitters, disorientation and a dry mouth.

Prevention

The only way to avoid a hangover completely is to not drink alcohol. However, presuming that you're not going to follow this bit of advice, at least heed these golden rules:

- Drink LOTS of water before and during the booze-up (try to drink alcohol on a 1:1 ratio with water).
- Eat – pasta, pizza and bread are particularly good, but all food will help.
- Don't mix drinks (that is, don't chase wine with shots, washed down by a pint of beer).
- Take a B vitamin before you drink.
- Don't smoke.

Cure

After extensive surveys and research (all conducted in the name of science), here are the top five hangover remedies:

H_2O: drink water. Drink, as much of it as you can.

Drink before you start with the alcohol, drink during the booze-up, and drink afterwards, before you go to sleep. Put a glass next to your bed and drink it when you wake up at 5.00 a.m. from the inevitable dreamy delirium. Then drink more when you finally crawl out of bed in the morning. It's the only way to cure your dehydration, and, although your stomach may feel like it will reject anything you pour down there, your body will thank you in the end.

Fry up: it turns out that there is scientific reason as to why a fry-up helps, aside from the fact that it tastes good. Firstly, the food will speed up your metabolism so that you break down the alcohol more quickly, as well as replacing some of the vital nutrients the alcohol flushed out. The salt (which you're likely to add to your chips) and egg are particularly good at doing this, and the fructose in the accompanying orange juice is good at burning up the alcohol. The arguments over tea and coffee are fierce, as caffeine will dehydrate you further. However, most people believe that the extra kick they give you will fight the headache and wake you up, and are worth you having to neck another pint of water.

....

NB: there are healthier foods that may be more effective in curing a hangover (bananas and fresh ginger, for example), but let's face it, when it's the morning after, the stomach will only entertain so much.

....

Exercise: people who exercise a lot tend to suffer milder hangovers than the unfit because their body flushes through the alcohol much faster. Exercise the next morning, however, is also a good thing as it gets your blood pumping, which will put the alcohol on the move. And, for some reason, a cold blast of air can do wonders, too.

Hair of the dog: following alcohol with more alcohol – can it really work? The principle is that it fulfils the craving your body has from having overdosed on it, in a small enough dose not to do too much further harm, although some argue it just delays the symptoms. Controversial, but lots of people swear by it, so try at your own risk.

And the most favoured drink is:

The Bloody Mary
- Vodka
- Tomato juice
- Lemon
- Worcestershire sauce
- Tabasco sauce
- Salt and pepper
- Celery
- Ice

... of course, it may be the juice and salt that's helping, rather than the vodka, but it's just not the hair of the dog without it.

Bed rest: let's face it, when you just can't face it, stay in bed. Time cures everything.

....

NB: there is also a range of painkillers (good for the headache) and 'hangover cures' available at the pharmacy – try at your discretion.

....

Girl stuff

(Boys may want to look away now.)

THE SMEAR TEST

Once you hit the age of 20, or when you start having sex (whichever is sooner), like a curse from an evil fairy, you inherit the drag of the three-yearly smear. A smear test is a method of cervical screening aimed at preventing cervical cancer by detecting and treating early signs.

Nobody actually *likes* the smear test – at least nobody I know. It's embarrassing, it's uncomfortable (it requires a bikini wax beforehand), but it's important not to miss. Usually, you will automatically be sent an invitation by the NHS to have a free smear test (lucky you). However, if you fall into the above categories and have not had one recently, you can (and should) request one from your GP, gynaecologist, Family Planning Clinic or Sexual Health Clinic.

THE BREAST CHECK

No, boys, this is not simply girls feeling themselves up. It's important for girls to check their breasts regularly (once a month) so that they can detect any changes that could be early signs of problems such as breast cancer.

Girls, pick a regular time each month (at the end of your period is best), and examine your breasts both through look and feel. You are looking for changes in size or shape; unusual lumps; puckering of the skin; and scabbing or discharging nipples. Check all the way from your armpit to your collarbone. If you find anything at all suspicious, don't panic, but do make an appointment with your GP.

Your GP, clinic or gynaecologist should also give you a clinical breast examination when you have your smear test and women aged 50–70 are offered a free screening every three years. These however, are not substitutes for self-examination.

THRUSH

OK, no beating around the bush (excuse the pun). Basically, thrush is itching, discharge and soreness – down there. It's not necessarily sexually transmitted, as it is caused by a fungus that can often be found in perfectly healthy people. It usually strikes when your body's normal defence mechanisms are down, like after a cold or flu, and can be easily treated by creams or tablets available from your doctor or pharmacist.

....

NB: if you have recurrent thrush, it's worthwhile for your partner to be treated too, as he could be carrying the infection without symptoms, and be passing it back to you.

....

Boy stuff

OK, boys – it's not just the girls who've got checks to do. There are important health issues that boys should be aware of as well. Below are some of the most common:

PROSTATE, TESTICULAR AND COLON CANCER

Prostate cancer is the most common cancer in men, although there are very few early symptoms. It's therefore important to have regular screening; although this is especially important after the age of 65, when it becomes more likely, it's also important in young men too. Much less talked about is **colon cancer**, but this is also a serious issue for men and requires regular screening. Talk to your GP about what tests are necessary for you. **Testicular cancer** is most common for younger men (aged around 15–40), particularly if there's a family history of the disease. Fortunately, self-examination can help to detect the disease early:

The testicle test

Pick a regular day each month and, after a hot bath or shower, feel your testicles with your thumb, index and middle fingers. You are checking for lumps; if you find one, you should make an urgent appointment with your GP. Other symptoms include: a dull ache in the abdomen or groin, and pain or discomfort in the testicle or scrotum.

HEART DISEASE

This is the biggest killer of men. However, heart disease can be easily monitored by regular checks of blood pressure (annually starting around the age of 21) and cholesterol (every few years from around the age of 35). You can help combat it through healthy eating and regular exercise.

IMPOTENCE AND LOSS OF LIBIDO

If you have lost your mojo, don't be embarrassed, even Austin Powers had his off day. And actually, this is a fairly common thing for men to experience at some point in their lives. It can be caused by a huge range of factors (for example: depression, stroke, alcohol, high blood pressure, drugs), and can be treated in many ways. Talk to your GP or clinic about what's the best treatment for you.

Infections

If you think you might have an STI, the first thing to do is to have a test. You will then either regain peace of mind or at least be able to start treatment straight away. The most common symptoms of STIs include: unusual genital discharge; a burning sensation when urinating; pain during sex; genital itching, rashes, or lumps. However, some STIs have no symptoms at all, so if you've had unprotected sex, you should have a check-up to be sure.

There are special sexual health clinics (also called GUM – genito-urinary medicine clinics) where you can go to be tested, if you're more comfortable there than at your GP or FPC. (Of course, then there's the old problem of seeing someone you know at a GUM. But just remember: if they're there long enough to spot you, then they're there for a reason too.) GUMs are usually located in hospitals, as part of a health centre, or as an individual clinic (ask NHS Direct to tell you where to find your nearest one). They're completely confidential and deal with STIs, contraception and pregnancy, cystitis and genital infections. Services include testing, general check-ups, treatment and counselling.

The paperwork

As with everything in life, there's always paperwork to keep track of and, as tedious as it can be, it's worth using a bit of stealth with your health:

HEALTH INSURANCE

If you're using the NHS, most of your treatment will be free. However, unless you're exempt, you may have to pay for things such as dental costs, opticians and prescriptions. One method to avoid this, if you can afford it, is to buy health insurance – it's like crash cover for your body instead of your car. Search for health insurance as you would for any other business: in the Yellow Pages, on the Internet, or through recommendations.

RECORDS
Medical card

This card contains your personal details, but most importantly, your NHS number. This is a number unique to you and is attached to all your medical records. It helps doctors to keep track of your medical history and is like a membership number for the NHS. You may be asked for it when joining a new surgery or clinic and, if you've lost your card, you can find out what it is by asking your previous GP or your Primary Care Trust's Patient and Practitioners Service Agency.

Injections

It's important to keep a note of every injection you've ever had, including your childhood ones, so that doctors will know what to give you. It can be dangerous to have the same injection twice within a certain period of time, but some injections are essential and need to be administered quickly. Write down the exact name of each injection, when you had it, and where. Then keep that piece of paper.

Illnesses and injury

You can become immune to some illnesses (for example chickenpox) once you've had them, so it's good to know what you have and haven't had. That way you can take care of baby Henry's chickenpox while everyone else stays well away. It's also important to know what you've had so that doctors can build up an idea of your medical history when treating current problems. Keep a record of all your illnesses and injuries, and ask your parents/ guardian for a list of your childhood diseases.

Blood type

This can be important to know if you need a blood transfusion, or if you want to give blood. Doctors can, of course, test your blood to find out your type, but it could save crucial time if you know it already.

Donor card

Not everyone wants to donate their organs, but if you do, make sure that you carry a donor card with you. It's a morbid thought, but the time spent finding out from your family whether or not you want to remain intact once dead could be the difference between life and death for someone else.

Health insurance

Keep a copy of your health insurance policy (with customer reference number and helpline) to hand. Health emergencies don't allow time to riffle through stacks of disorganised folders, or search through the stuffed filing cabinet that is last season's handbag.

Travel and injections

So, you're registered everywhere, you've got your specialists on speed-dial, you know exactly which pharmacist is the best and who to go to when you have what illness ... what happens when you go away? When travelling, there are three important health issues to consider:

TRAVEL INSURANCE

You need to make sure that you will be eligible for immediate medical treatment, should you need it, wherever you go. To do this, you need travel insurance. It can add to your travel costs, and although it might not seem as important as covering your wallet, which is more likely to go missing than your spleen, when you weigh it all up, covering your leg/liver/head/[insert relevant body part here] is probably more essential should the odds strike.

INJECTIONS

Many exotic locations boast, along with their exotic beaches, exotic diseases too. Find out from your GP or local travel clinic what injections, if any, you need, and make sure you do this far enough in advance of your trip for the injections to take effect (usually two weeks is enough).

Medical kit

When you're away, the chances are that you will not find yourself being rushed to a hospital. However, you could easily suffer some minor accident or illness, and might discover that saying 'paracetemol' in Chinese is not so easy. So, make sure you take with you the bare essentials.

Essential medical kit:

- Plasters
- Tweezers
- Antiseptic cream
- Cotton wool
- Paracetemol
- Imodium/Dioralite
- Sting cream

- Calamine lotion
- Antihistamine cream
- Thermometer
- Ice pack
- Stomach settler
- Bug spray
- Sunscreen

And that's about it, folks. You should now be completely competent in all manner of health trifles and major emergencies. You can thus roll your eyes when your friends don't know what to do, shake your head when someone arrives at A&E with the flu, and confidently say 'Of *course* you need to go to casualty' when your boyfriend rocks up with a gash in his head. If, however, after all of this extensive advice, you get ill, or have to look after someone who's ill, and *still* don't have a clue what to do, maybe put the ambulance on speed-dial, and, please, don't take up a career as a doctor.

3

MOVING OUT: THE PROPERTY PREDICAMENT

Moving out of home can be a long and confusing business, with a lot to think about beyond simply paying rent. When my friend Sophie triumphantly moved out of home, she waved goodbye to her parents smug in the knowledge that never again would she have to hear the words: 'So long as you live under my roof, you'll live by my rules.'

Gleefully she invited over her boyfriend Duncan –
who at the age of 25 was finally allowed to sleep in her
room – she made herself exactly what she wanted for
dinner, she decided on a whim to watch a movie at three
in the morning, she smoked *inside* the flat, and she called
in a sickie the next day to revel in her new-found nest.

But, the day after that, a storm began. At around six
o'clock in the evening, Sophie noticed an obnoxious
drip forcing its way through the bedroom ceiling. By
seven, the bucket she'd placed underneath it was full, so
were the five mugs, two bowls and one ashtray that were
now forming a mystic circle around her room, and by
eight, a patch in the ceiling, directly above her bed,
collapsed. Sophie eyed the mess that was covering her
dream bed and decided that she would not crumble like
the roof had done. She would stick it out until morning,
call the insurance company, and get the roof repaired.
Then she remembered that she didn't yet have insurance.

Panicking, she began to tear through the Yellow
Pages for a cheap roofer, but, ten minutes later, the
power went off. Then the rats arrived. And since Sophie
didn't have a cat, Duncan was on holiday and the Pied
Piper was unavailable, Sophie called her dad.

Smilingly he welcomed her into the car and when
they reached the house, Sophie, calming down at last, lit
up a cigarette. Then her mum appeared. 'Sophie,' she
said. 'You're not smoking are you? You know, so long as
you live under our roof …'

Of course, not all property experiences have to be as traumatic as Sophie's (who, by the way, is now living comfortably in her own dry, rat-free, and completely insured home). And if trauma does arise, there's a lot you can do to make sure that these property problems remain safely locked out.

Finding a home

Your first property is more likely to be rented than bought with a mortgage, so that's what I've focused on here. However, most of the following information relates to both. The basic difference is: your landlord is responsible for repairing things if you rent, whereas if you buy, you are responsible for everything.

REQUIREMENTS

When looking for a property to rent, the first thing to consider is what your requirements are and what is feasible within your budget. (There's no point listing a swimming pool, personal race track and cinema room in your requirements – no matter how good they look on MTV Cribs – if your budget is more suited to a paddling pool and six-inch TV.)

The main factors to take into account are: budget, location, local amenities, space, facilities and garden. However, choosing a property is a very individual affair and different aspects will carry more weight for different people. For example, if you are a commuter, bear in mind how close you need to be to the nearest tube. And if you are a light sleeper, bear in mind that trains, while convenient, are also noisy. The best thing to do is to make a list of all the factors that will play a role in your day-to-day life and then try to prioritise them in terms of importance. For example, would you prefer more space somewhere out of town where the height of glamour is the local pub, or a tiny hovel in the heart of the city buzz?

ESTATE AGENTS

The next thing to do is either trawl through the local papers in the area in which you wish to rent, or find an estate agent who will do the trawling for you – for a fee, of course. Sometimes you will be able to deal with the landlord direct but most often you will have to go through an estate agent at some point, the difference being whether you pick an agent to find you a property, or you pick a property and talk to its agent. If you decide to start with an agent, you can either go to one agent (who, if you use exclusively, might give you a higher level of attention) or multiple agents (who will plague you with phone calls but provide you with a wider breadth of choice). Each of them will try to match a property with your personal requirements and show you everything they think is suitable. (Estate agents can be found in the local paper, in the

Yellow Pages, on the Internet, or by walking down the high street.)

VIEWING

This is the next necessity. Agents will liaise with the current owners to arrange a time for you to 'view' the property and will often line up a range of properties for you to look at in one day. This is a good idea because, although it's tiring and means you having to forgo the *Hollyoaks* omnibus and the latest instalment of *The O.C.*, it means you can make a direct comparison between different places, hopefully aiding your decision.

Some properties are rented 'site-unseen' (that is, you don't actually go and see it) but this is risky business as smooth salesmen and flashy photography can lead you to believe you're renting quite a different fairy-tale castle from the dungeon you arrive at. Your own eyes are the safest judge – along with your sense of smell, hearing and touch when you're testing for water pressure and damp.

Hold on, I see you raising your eyebrows. Did no one tell you about looking for damp? OK, you may not be renting this place for life (if you were, I'd be giving you a much longer list), but even when viewing a property to rent, there is a range of BEWARE signs to look out for:

Damp: look at all the walls and ceilings in the property and check for signs of damp (dark patches that look like spilt coffee, or lovely clumps of mould). Damp is a problem. It will ruin your paintwork and could mean that the building has structural issues causing bigger problems, so don't ignore it, even if the estate agent is really good-looking and smiling disarmingly – this is not the time to let your eyes go gooey, because if they do, so will the walls.

Water pressure: some properties, especially if they're high up, will have poor water pressure. This means that when you step into the sparkling new power shower that was the main reason you were attracted to the bathroom in the first place, you will discover that the power in the shower is no more. In fact, to describe it as a 'shower' at all is misleading. What you're having is a 'trickle'. So, make sure you check this out, *before* the deal is done. Simply turn on the taps and the showerhead and see how fast the water spouts. And don't worry, it's not rude – you're allowed to do things like this. After all, you wouldn't buy a car without a test drive.

Windows: check the windows for crumbling/rotting sides and also for double-glazing, as windows will play a big role in keeping in the heat (thus keeping your bills down), and keeping out the noise – particularly important if the building is on a busy road.

Roof: if there's anything wrong with the roof, it can have a catalogue of side effects and could be very expensive for your landlord to fix – which often means that he won't. So, it's important to look at it for any irregularities. Now, I know that if you're reading this section, you're probably not a property surveyor and don't know all that much about roofs, but don't worry, I'm not expecting you to take a course in engineering. What you're looking for here is a comparison – it's just like a game of 'spot the difference'. Basically, compare the roof on your property to that on the neighbour's. Is yours slanting excessively? Has it lost many slates? Is the guttering falling off? And, most tellingly, does your neighbour have a new roof? If so, it's likely that your property will need a new roof very soon as well, since the chances are your properties will have been built at the same time. If you notice something like this, ask a few more questions.

Heating: the first thing to do is check to see if the property has a central heating system. If it doesn't, you'll need to get either some electric heaters – which will add to your electricity bill – or invest in some serious winter woolies. If there is heating, test the radiators to see if they're working, and have a look at the boiler. We'll get into detail about boilers a bit later on, but what you're really looking at here is the age of the system. If it's rusty, making a whole lot of noise, and leaking a puddle of water, it probably means there'll be a few bumps on the way to warmth.

Noise: you may think this won't be a problem for you, but even the most hard-core of partiers have to sleep sometimes, and you won't be happy if your hard-earned snooze is interrupted by a blaring TV from next door, or by the clanging of bottles at the bottle-bank you hadn't noticed across the street. So, use your ears and listen. And if you can, try to visit the property at different times of day – what might appear to be a quiet suburban road at two-thirty in the afternoon, might not seem so tranquil come rush hour.

....

NB: don't let the estate agent keep talking so that every possible sound is drowned out.

....

Ask questions

Don't be afraid of asking questions. Showing that you know what you're looking for gives the estate agent a sign that you mean business and won't be a pushover when it comes to negotiating price. Plus, there are some pretty important questions to ask. For example:

Service charge: this is a fee for the maintenance, cleaning, and gardening of communal areas, so if the property is in a block, there's likely to be a service charge. Sometimes this is included in the rent, but most often it's not, and will sneakily strike from nowhere, leaving you stunned and staring at your empty bank balance before you've even finished moving in. So, ask if there's a service charge and make sure it's within your budget.

MAKING AN OFFER

Once you've found a property that you want to rent, the next stage is to make an offer to the landlord. There is some leeway at this point for negotiating rent, especially if you're able to move in quickly, as a landlord would generally rather have a property rented at a slightly lower rate, than have it stand empty with no rent at all. However, if there's a lot of competition for the property, it's best to put in an offer close to the asking price so that you give the landlord as little as possible to consider, and no reason to look to anyone else.

Other aspects that make you an attractive tenant are:

- Having a job (making you more likely to be able to pay the rent).
- Showing that you will take pride in the place and are capable of taking some responsibility in looking after it (making it less likely that you'll take to playing darts on the wall).
- Not being too pushy (a landlord won't want a tenant who is on their back day and night expecting the flat to work like the Plaza when the rent wouldn't cover a coffee in the Plaza).

Unfortunately, your word is not enough to prove any of the above so be prepared to provide references. (Most landlords will want to make sure that you are not a raving psychopath, you haven't just escaped from jail, and you didn't burn your last flat down.)

At this stage, your offer is not legally binding and both you and the landlord can still pull out of the deal. However, you will probably be asked to provide a certain amount of rent up front (usually one week's worth), which acts as a holding deposit to hold the agreement while the official paperwork is being drawn up.

CONTRACTS

You will then be asked to sign the tenancy agreement. This is the contract between you and the landlord that lays out all the terms of the agreement between you, such as the price, the length of tenancy and who is responsible for what.

....

NB: you will generally find that the section about the responsibilities of the landlord is very small – he basically agrees to let you live in the property and fix things that break – whereas your responsibilities as the tenant are far more extensive. You must do this, you can't do that, you must never do the other. Don't worry though – this is standard, a lot of the rules will never be enforced, and if there's one that really grates, the landlord might be willing to remove it.

....

The most important thing to look out for is the stipulation about how much notice you have to give the landlord before you leave, and how much notice he needs to give you before chucking you out, should the circumstance arise. This is called a **break clause** and is important, as you need to make sure that you will always be given enough time to find a new place before you are made homeless. You also need to make sure that you won't be trapped into a long contract making you unable to leave when you want. If you're renting through a reputable estate agent, they should be able to advise you on anything you don't understand in the contract. However, if in doubt, they should at least be able to recommend a solicitor who will advise you about all the ins and outs.

INVENTORY

With contracts signed it's almost time to move in, but before you do so, an inventory will probably be carried out. This is basically a list of everything in the property, noting the condition it's in before you start your tenancy. In essence, it's a way of making sure you don't nick anything when you move out, or destroy anything while you're there.

NB: this 'check-in' inventory will usually be paid for by the landlord, but you will be expected to pay for the inventory on the 'check-out' when you leave, unless otherwise agreed.

A copy of the inventory should be sent to both you

and the landlord. Make sure it is and that you check it carefully, because, although it should have been carried out by an independent inventory clerk, you don't want to find yourself held liable for paintwork/carpeting/a wide-screen TV, if these things weren't in place when you moved in.

PAYMENT

OK, this is where you have to get your wallet out. With everything agreed, it's time to cough up the rent. You'll usually be expected to pay one month's rent in advance, as well as a deposit (generally about six weeks' rent) that you'll get back at the end of the tenancy, so long as you don't destroy the place in the interim. This is very annoying, but instead of cursing as the landlord pulls the money out of your clenched fist, remember, this arrangement can work for you too. The landlord is responsible for everything, not you. So, when you get a leak, or a power cut, or rats, or a faulty dishwasher, call the landlord. He gets the money – you get to be annoying!

EXTRAS

Now for the extra money: if you used an estate agent at the start, this is when they will ask you for a fee to cover administration costs. I know what you're thinking: 'I'm paying the landlord, the inventory geezer, two-and-a-half months' rent up front, and now I have to pay the estate agent too!' Well, yes, sorry. But don't forget that they did find you the property, draw up all the paper-work and seal the deal, so it's probably worth it in the long run, just don't be surprised when it hits you.

Once this money has been cleared and everything has been signed, it's over. You can finally collect your keys (admiring the jangle that tells the world you have moved on and up!), settle into your new home, and dream of all the things you have to look forward to – like food shopping, vacuuming and paying the bills.

BUYING REQUIREMENTS

The requirements for renting a property still apply here, but buying a property is much more of a serious business than renting because it deals with serious money and serious commitment. Costs can accrue long before the deal is done, and there's a whole stack of extras to think about. Here are some of the most important:

- **Viewing:** be extra vigilant in looking for flaws and asking questions as you will now be the one who bears the cost of any oversights.
- **Leasehold/freehold:** find out if you will own the property outright, or just for a fixed period of time. This will affect your rights and responsibilities, as well as the property price.
- **Length of lease:** anything less than 65–70 years might lead to difficulties in securing a mortgage, or selling the property on.

- **Homebuyer's survey:** get this before you buy, and study the report carefully as it will assess the real state of the property. It will be an extra cost, but if you're getting a mortgage, the mortgage lender will require you to have at least a basic survey conducted of the property anyway, which could alert you to hidden problems.
- **Solicitor's fees:** you need a solicitor when buying a property. The fees will include the solicitor's expertise and advice, as well as the local authority search, the landlord's registration fee, the land registration fee, and so on, which will all be necessary before the deal can complete.
- **Mortgage:** you can either go to a mortgage lender direct, or to a mortgage broker who will advise you on which mortgage to pick. Some charge, others won't, so check first.
- **Stamp duty:** is a crafty property tax that is unavoidable, unless your property falls below a certain price bracket, so factor it in when working out your budget.

Once your offer has been accepted, you will 'exchange', that is, you and the vendor both sign the contract and you pay a deposit. A date for 'completion' will then be set, where you pay the rest of the money and, finally, get the keys.

BILLS, BILLS, BILLS!

Moving into your own home has lots of advantages:

independence, freedom and a free run of the house. However, it also has many disadvantages: you are independently responsible for paying the rent, you have the freedom to leave the TV blaring so long as you keep up with the electricity bill, and you have free run of the house so long as you understand that absolutely nothing is free. In fact, there's a whole catalogue of bills that you may not have even considered:

Council tax

This varies depending on the value of your property and also the area in which you live, but it's likely to be a considerable fee. Sometimes it's included in the price of rent, but often it's not, and the most annoying thing about this tax is that it's your responsibility to inform the council that you need to start paying it. If you don't, and they find out later, it will be considered a serious offence. So, call or write to the council, tell them you are now living in your new property, and, like clockwork, faster than you've ever seen the council achieve anything before, you'll start receiving your bills. However, there may be a range of discounts that you are eligible for (for example if you're a student or are elderly) so make sure to ask the council for information about this.

Utilities

So, I'm presuming you want to receive gas, water, a

phone line and electricity. You therefore need to pay for these things and will have to find out who the suppliers are for your property. Sometimes you can pick and choose, but other times there will already be one established for your building, and it could be a hassle to change it.

The landlord (if you are renting) may make arrangements for you, but he should at least be able to tell you who to contact. Simply call each of the suppliers, inform them that you are the new tenant at the address, and start up a new account – you don't want to be held liable for outstanding bills. However, if for some reason the landlord can't track down this information (and peering through neighbours' letterboxes to sneak a peak at who's sending them their electricity bills isn't working), there are some overarching utility regulators who will be able to tell you who your supplier is (see Chapter 10, Useful Contacts).

Insurance

Although a hefty cost, insuring your home is absolutely essential, on a basic level at least. It can be split into two categories: home building insurance and home contents insurance. The first refers to the structure of the building itself, but the landlord should have this one covered (although you will need this if buying a property). What you need to be concerned about is the contents: basically, everything that would fall out if you turned your house upside down and shook it. As you are likely to underestimate this, it's worth making a list with a value for each item. The contents should be covered for loss and damage, but the price will vary considerably depending on the value of what you're insuring. Just make sure that that if there's anything of particular value in your home (for example jewellery, a computer, or a big TV) it's named specifically in your policy.

TV licence

There's little chance that you could fail to notice the fact that you have to pay for a TV licence because the helpful people who issue them will probably have sent you three reminders and a letter threatening that they will 'always find you' before you've even had a chance to take the TV out of its box. However, if somehow you've managed to escape this rain of post, simply go to your local post office and pay your TV licence there. Yes, it's an annoying extra cost, but definitely better than the fine you have to pay if you're caught without one.

Resident's permit

If you have a car but don't have off-street parking, the chances are you're going to have to buy a resident's permit. For this you'll need to contact the council (again!). You will also need to search through your yet-unpacked boxes and locate your driving licence, your vehicle registration document, and proof of residence at your new property (such as your tenancy agreement or a council tax bill). The snag of course is that each of these documents must show your new address and, since you've just moved in, it's unlikely that you will have been so efficient as to have already changed the address on your driving licence. Fortunately, you can usually get a temporary permit from the council, which gives you a few months to sort out all your address changes, and then go through the whole process again.

Getting settled

You should now have successfully rented a property, moved in, paid your bills, and, in all fairness, you should be able to sit back with a cup of tea boiled with the electricity you've paid for, in the chair you manoeuvred up three flights of stairs, and enjoy the tranquillity of your very own home. Unfortunately, it's quite likely that, before the week is out, the chair will break, the electricity will blow, or the water will mockingly turn brown. Don't panic. Things will always break, but with a little extra knowledge, they needn't be broken for long.

PLUMBING

The key to plumbing and electrics is in understanding just enough about them to know when you need a plumber or electrician, and when you can save the call-out fee/hassle and do it yourself. So, here are the basics:

Central heating systems

The first thing to do is find out whether your system is a combi-boiler or a regular boiler with tank. A combi-boiler heats water instantly and is more efficient because, as it doesn't store hot water in a tank, none is wasted. However, due to this same tanklessnes, and the fact that there isn't an excess of stored water, it means that you may have problems using more than one tap at a time. This isn't a problem if you're living alone (and always a fun game to turn on the kitchen tap when someone else is in the shower), but if there's a lot of people in the property, all jostling for hot baths, a tank-operated boiler is probably better.

The important things to locate are the time clock and the thermostat – ask your landlord where these things are. Often, if you're suddenly not getting hot water, the solution will be as simple as flicking the power back on or adjusting the thermostat, so always check these before calling the plumber. You should also know where the mains stopcock is, so that if there's a leak you can isolate it. And if you have a combi-boiler, make sure you charge it once in a while. (If you notice the gauge going low, simply open the valve and this will charge it up.)

For anything more complicated than this, it's probably a good idea to contact your landlord, who will arrange for a plumber to visit. However, ask the landlord where the pump and valves are so that you can direct the plumber to them – sometimes they're very difficult to find and can even be located under floorboards.

....

NB: if your radiators are on, but not heating up properly, it may simply be that you have an air-block and need to 'bleed' the radiator. To do this, use a spanner or radiator key to twist the hexagonal nut on the side of your radiator. If there is an air-block, you'll hear the air hissing out. Once the air has been removed, the water should flow through again and the radiator work. If water comes out instead, this means that the problem isn't an air-block.

....

Unblocking the sink/toilet

Toilet: you'll know your toilet is blocked when the flush begins to die or when the bowl overflows. Unblocking it is probably the most disgusting job you will have to deal with in your new home. There's no getting away from it and no way to escape the yuck beyond putting a peg over your nose, grabbing a plunger and donning very thick rubber gloves.

....

NB: a toilet brush should not be used as a plunger. This is for cleaning, not unclogging and will result in a very messy brush – and probably a toilet that remains blocked.

....

Basically, you're trying to dislodge whatever is

causing the blockage. You do this by prodding it enough so that it breaks into flushable pieces, and by creating a vacuum that sucks it back up. So, once festooned in your armour, the first step is to bail out the excess water, leaving just enough to cover the plunger cup which should be placed over the drain opening. You then need a rapid push-and-pull action, a good arm, and a strong stomach. After pumping for about ten times, yank the plunger up, and hopefully a myriad of different-sized bits of waste will rise up into the bowl. If they don't, repeat the process and then flush.

If, however, flushing causes the bowl to flood again – the toilet is not yet fully unclogged. First of all – and quickly – remove the top of the cistern and close the flush valve by hand. You then need to bail out the water and start the process again.

Sink: the sink follows a similar principle, but is far less disgusting. Using a sink plunger (not the dirty toilet plunger!), place the plunger-cup over the plughole. If your sink has a second basin or overflow, plug this with an old dishcloth or rag. Now pump in short, rapid movements just as you did with the toilet, and repeat until the blockage is clear.

Electrics

There are really only two essentials that you need to be familiar with when it comes to electrics: the meter and the fuse box. For anything more complicated than this, or if you have a power-cut, call your electricity supplier. DON'T start trying to solve electrical issues yourself, or you might get a bigger shock than the cost of the electrician.

Most new fuse boxes will have circuit breakers so that if the circuit overloads, the relevant switch will flick off. (Often this will happen if you have too many electrics on the go at the same time.) All you need then do is turn one of the electrical items off and flick the switch back on. If this doesn't work, you may need to replace the fuse, and then flick the switch. Older systems, however, will just have the fuses themselves, without switches, which means you have to test each one to find out which fuse has blown. You can do this by taking each fuse out and looking for the broken wire. When you locate the correct fuse, simply replace it with a new one, and then turn the power back on.

....

NB: before attempting to change a fuse, BE CAREFUL. Make sure that all appliances on the overloaded circuit are unplugged and that the main switch (or breaker) is turned to the off position. Remember to take a torch with you and make sure that your hands are dry and there's no moisture on the floor. Ensure you've selected the right kind of fuse for your particular circuit (for lights, usually 3–5A is OK, for larger appliances, a larger one), and that it's tightly screwed in. Then turn the power back on – and behold, there is light.

....

The meter can be located in lots of different places, so make sure the landlord tells you where it is before you move in. To read the meter, simply read off the numbers, omitting the last one or two digits which will be a different colour from the rest. Sometimes the electricity man will actually visit the building to read the meter, but frequently your supplier will give you the choice of reading the meter yourself, or accepting their estimation of how much electricity you use. ALWAYS read it yourself, as they are more than likely to conveniently overestimate.

Changing a plug

This is one of those tasks that you know is dead easy to do, but if you've never been taught how to do it, is as easy as reading Greek. So, prepare to become a plug expert in two minutes flat:

1. First of all, use a screwdriver to unscrew the middle screw on the front of the plug, which should then allow the cover to come off. Inside, the plug will look like this:

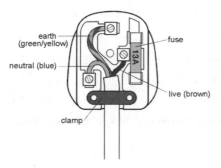

earth (green/yellow)

fuse

neutral (blue)

13A

live (brown)

clamp

2. The brown wire is connected to the fuse, the green-and-yellow wire is the earth wire, and the blue wire is neutral. The clamp at the bottom simply stops the wires from coming out when pulled and can be adjusted by tightening or loosening the two remaining screws on the front of the plug. To change the plug, simply unscrew each of the wires, then screw them back into the same position in the new plug, always remembering to earth it. Alternatively, if you're changing only the fuse, simply snap the fuse out and put the new one in.
3. Once this has been done you can replace the cover, screw it back on, and you're done. You have successfully changed a plug and are officially an electrical whiz!

Breakages

Should anything else in your home break (like a door handle, cabinet hinge or chair leg), and if you don't happen to have a handy friend who can fix things, a handyman is the best person to call. You can find one in the Yellow Pages or through recommendation, but make sure you agree a fee before he comes out.

Neighbours – a little understanding

Perhaps the only thing you can't control in your property, even if you are an electrician, plumber and mortgage broker all rolled into one, is the temperament of your neighbours. Now, your neighbours might be the friendliest, most amicable and understanding people in the world. They might ply you with brownies and cupcakes, ward vagrants away from your car, or be highly placed in the film industry and invite you to a catalogue of glittering premiers. However, they might also be loud, smelly, aggressive, territorial and assault you with letters, post-it notes or, even worse, angry red faces should you so much as breathe on their lawn. Unfortunately, there's not much you can do about it, other than be your lovely, smiling, yet not-prepared-to-be-bullied, self.

The key is to try to build up a relationship with them and keep the channels for communication open, so that if either of you feel grieved, you can simply tell the other, instead of letting it build up until you find a voodoo doll hammered to your front door. One tip is to invest in a sturdy pair of earplugs. Another is to warn your neighbours in advance if you're the one planning any building work, parties or other unusually loud activities, so at least they won't be startled when their walls start shaking, and have the opportunity to book themselves a day out.

However, if, no matter what you do, they can't be appeased – or if you find that they're the ones constantly making noise and their empty promises will no longer appease you – the next step for you is to speak to the council, or in very extreme cases contact the police. But be warned – involving the authorities will probably increase hostility and make things worse for you for a while; eviction can take a very, very long time.

Some final property pointers

- Give yourself time. Finding and renting a property can be very time-consuming and almost always takes longer than you had thought.
- If you're splitting costs with a flat-mate friend, make sure you have a properly agreed arrangement (preferably in writing) that covers all the fees, so that you don't lose either money or friendship when it becomes time to pay the bills.
- Make sure you look after your keys; a disadvantage of living on your own is that no one else will be inside to open the door should you forget them. If, however, you do lose your keys: call a locksmith, sit on your doorstep for two hours until he arrives (most likely in the midst of winter), pay for him to change the locks and give you a new key – then give a spare set to a responsible friend, one who won't lose the keys himself.

4
PLAYING HOUSE

When we were about 18, my friend Lisa's parents went on holiday for a month. Of course, they had no idea that their home would soon become synonymous with the word 'house-party'. Every night for four weeks we piled into Lisa's house, and every day there were at least four or five stragglers lounging around, eating food, dropping crumbs and forgetting to wipe their feet. Yes, we noticed the fuzz growing out of the soup we had spilled over the hob weeks earlier, we observed the growing mound of plates, bowls and glasses forming a balancing act in the sink, and we did wonder what the smell coming out of the bathroom could be. But we decided to leave it until the end and promised that we'd all pitch in and help her clean up before her parents arrived home. After all, we figured, how hard could it be?

Two carpets full of holes, one flooded toilet and one discoloured coffee table later we discovered the answer: pretty damn hard. Now, some of us had cleaned before. We all vaguely knew how to operate a vacuum cleaner (although no one quite figured out what to do when the suction stopped), most of us discovered we were quite skilled at dusting, and someone even remembered that bleach was necessary to clean the loo. But beyond that, our expertise was limited. No one realised that bleach, while good at getting marks out of the white sink, was not so efficient at cleaning the blue carpet. No one knew that using half a can of polish on the mirror would not leave a happy reflection. And no one mentioned that it was going to be difficult to get rid of the smell of three-week-old smoke.

We cleaned for an entire day. And when Lisa's mum walked into the house that night, it took her exactly 24 seconds to remark, 'Lisa, what *have* you been doing in this house?'

The moral of this story is: it's not as easy as it looks. Cleaning is not merely about donning rubber gloves and waving a duster around. There's a lot to learn, and when done properly, it's an art form. Fortunately, however, we don't all have to be the polishing Picasso, and most people can learn the basics fairly fast. So, here they are, the basics (gleaned from the advice of the most snooty of cleaning connoisseurs):

Housework – man versus dust

Be organised and you will be surprised how much easier housework can be.

PREPARATION

So, imagine you're about to take part in a Premiership football match. What's the first thing you do? (Besides phoning all your mates to tell them you have suddenly acquired the skills of a superstar footballer.) You put on your kit. Well, cleaning is the same deal. Preparation is essential. You need: kit, tools and tactics.

Kit

OK, so this isn't quite as swanky as a football strip. Basically, all we're really talking about is rubber gloves, clothes you don't mind dirtying and comfy shoes. The gloves are important, though, as you're going to be touching a range of products, some of which can burn your skin. And since you might also be combating germ-infested zones, like the underside of the toilet lid, trust me, you'll be glad of a bit of protection.

Tools

You will need:

- Vacuum cleaner
- Mop
- Bucket
- Two sponges
- Duster
- Squeegee
- Three soft cloths (one for products, one for water, one dry)
- Polish
- Bleach
- Bathroom cleaner
- Antibacterial surface cleaner
- Glass cleaner
- Household ammonia or rubbing alcohol
- Rubber gloves

Tactics

The first thing to establish is your opening play. Where are you going to start? There's no set rule about this, but it's a good idea to start with the cleaning chores that could make a mess, rather than the ones designed to leave that finishing sparkle. So, don't vacuum the floor before doing the dusting, otherwise the lovely clean carpet will be left covered in dust. And don't buff the wooden staircase only to drip last night's casserole, leaking through the over-full bin bag, all over them. Try instead to work from the top down. Do all the potentially messy jobs first. Do all the heavy cleaning and scrubbing, do the toilets and sinks, the windows and rugs. And then, and only then, add the sparkle (generally found in a can of polish and a vacuum cleaner).

UNDERSTANDING THE CLEANING GAME

Before you can play the game, you have to understand the tactics. So, it's time for a quick run-down of how to carry out some of the most common cleaning tasks:

Windows

Before washing windows check the weather forecast to see whether or not the game has been cancelled. I know, it sounds like I'm taking this sports analogy too far now, but actually I'm not joking. Sunlight can cause windows to streak, and it also makes it difficult for you to see if you've cleaned all the watermarks or not. So, aim for a cloudy day, or sometime late in the afternoon.

The next thing to do is to prepare for spillage. I'm not saying you're not a window whiz, but everybody spills a little, so put an old towel on the windowsill to catch any drips before they reach the floor. Then, have a quick dust – focusing particularly on the window frame and sills. Next, reach for your bucket. If your windows are only slightly dirty, you can simply spray a glass-cleaner onto a soft cloth, avoiding much of the mess, but if your windows are so dirty that the world looks sepia, you're going to need to add a bit of ammonia to a vinegar-and-warm-water mix.

You can now start cleaning. Gently wipe your cloth horizontally across the window until the whole pane is covered. For a truly good clean, you'll need to follow this with a squeegee, but you can get away with a dry cloth if you don't have one. (Squeegees, however, make you feel like a fully bona fide window cleaner.) Work the squeegee (or dry cloth) downwards over the window, wiping the squeegee with a paper towel after each stroke to avoid putting the dirt back on the pane. You'll then be left with a small section at the bottom that's still dirty (because it's where your squeegee strokes stopped). Wipe this horizontally and then dry the windows with a clean dry cloth or rag.

You should now have clean and sparkling windows that you can actually see through! It's time to move on – remembering of course to pick up the towel and wipe down the windowsill and frame before you go.

Furniture

There are two major cleaning challenges that furniture presents: cleaning the furniture itself, and cleaning the floor/wall/pile of hidden rubbish it's blocking. Yes, I'm afraid that furniture is a huge dust trap and it must be moved – perhaps a good day to invite round a muscular friend. Neglect this dusting duty and you could find yourself face-to-face with a giant ball of dust the size of a small animal. You may also discover a patch of ground-in dirt on the floor that amazingly resembles the shape of your desk, and lungs that are rapidly beginning to sound asthmatic. So, dust often.

Of course, different types of furniture need to be treated differently, and remember to TEST everything first:

Wood: the best way to dust wood furniture is with a soft dry cloth and some furniture polish – dust may be tiny, but it's surprisingly strong and could scratch the surface if there's no polish to soften it. Use a circular motion and be sparing with the amount of polish you use. (Never use soap or water, as this can damage the wood.)

....

NB: remember to change dust cloths regularly – dirty ones may contain old dust or dirt that will scratch your furniture.

....

However, even with the greatest dusting care, inevitably there will be the odd spill, scratch or stain. The best piece of advice here is to act quickly, and blot, don't rub. For serious scratches or stains, you'll probably need to call in a professional wood cleaner, but for minor problems you can have a go yourself.

The first thing to do is to remove the spillage by carefully scooping (or vacuuming) off solids and blotting excess liquid. Once this has been done you'll have to assess the spill. For grease marks or streaky finishes, clean by rubbing with a solvent-containing furniture polish or an ammonia-and-water solution, and wipe with a clean, soft cloth. For water marks and minor scratches, use a paste wax and fine wool cloth. (As with all cleaning, remember to test your products on a small and inconspicuous part of the furniture item.)

....

NB: the best way to keep your furniture looking perfect is to prevent damage. So avoid placing furniture in direct sunlight (which can fade it), keep it away from extreme heat, and try not to change your brand of polish too often as this can make the wood look streaky.

....

Upholstery: as with wood, the most important tip is to dust and vacuum regularly. Be thorough and do all detachable parts (like sofa pillows) separately. This should be the extent of your cleaning most of time but occasionally you will have to do a more extensive job and actually wash the upholstery. Depending on how confident you feel in your housework wizardry, you might want to call in a professional. But if you're brave enough, here's how to do it yourself:

1. First of all vacuum the entire surface area. It's now time to prepare your magic potion. Mix (with an electric mixer) approximately $1/4$ cup of laundry detergent with 1 cup of warm water until it looks like foam. (Alternatively, you can buy a speciality upholstery cleaner.)
2. Dip a clean cloth in the mixture and gently rub the foam onto the fabric (remembering to pick an inconspicuous area first.) Use a clean, hard cloth to wipe the dirty foam away, then rinse the area with a damp cloth.
3. Repeat this over the entire surface, then allow to dry – if you sit on it too soon you are likely to leave a big mark, and get a wet bum.

For more concentrated stains – like spilled wine, ink, grease and the like – there's a more concentrated solution, but before you run for the wet cloth remember one word: RESIST. Yes, you must act fast, but not with excess water and not with frantic scrubbing.

1. Stop, breathe and blot. If, after you have blotted all the excess liquid (changing the face of the cloth each time it becomes dirty) there still remains a stain, you can now reach for the water – but sparingly.
2. Mix some warm water with a small amount of laundry detergent or rubbing alcohol and lightly dab onto the stain. DON'T use too much water as this can spread the stain and damage your upholstery.

3. Rinse with a damp (not wet), clean sponge and blot dry. Repeat until the stain has gone – or until you admit defeat, call in the professionals or turn the sofa cushion over. (If, when you turn the cushion over, you discover another long-forgotten stain, don't panic. Many a sofa looks particularly fetching when covered in a fancy – and handy – throw.)

Leather: follow the specific instructions that should come with your leather furniture, as these will be tailored to your particular item. However, for daily leather cleaning, dusting should be sufficient. Any spills should be blotted immediately, then left to dry naturally, and for anything too complicated – call in a professional.

Electrics

Computers, TVs and other electrics need to be cleaned just as much, and in fact, even more so than the rest of your furniture because if they are dusty or dirty, they can easily become damaged. Much electrical equipment will come with special cleaning products (or their instruction booklets will encourage you to go back to the shop and buy the special cleaning products) but normal household tools can be used too.

A soft cloth, dampened with a small amount of water or rubbing alcohol is the most crucial tool for cleaning and will generally be enough. Simply wipe it gently over the components to remove dust, and wipe the hard-to-reach areas with a moistened cotton or foam swab, such as a cotton bud. Vacuuming can be helpful as well – but be careful that the suction doesn't suck up any detachable parts. And remember to turn the electrics OFF before cleaning.

NB: DON'T use strong cleaning solvents, as these could react with the plastics used in your electrics. And DON'T spray water or any type of liquid directly onto the electrics (unless you want an electric shock and a broken machine). Don't leave your bucket of water near them either.

Floors

For those of you who grew up on a diet of Disney and will always picture Snow White happily sweeping and singing as she goes about her day – get real. It's not that fun. But if done regularly, it doesn't have to be a huge chore either. Your first task is easy: identify what kind of floor you're trying to clean:

Carpets (vacuuming): before vacuuming, pick up all the litter, dirty clothes and piles of clean laundry that have accumulated on the floor since you last forced yourself to tidy. Then try to remove any big pieces of dirt, fluff-balls, or hair-clumps that could clog up your vacuum. Once this is done, check that the vacuum bag isn't already full, as this will prevent suction. (Obviously, if it is full – change it.) You are now ready to vacuum.

There's no real set rule about how to do this. Some people go forwards, some go back, some even make circles. But however you do it, make sure that your strips overlap so that you don't miss a spot. And change the direction in which you vacuum every now and then so that your carpet maintains its bounce and doesn't lie flat and lifeless.

When the time comes that no amount of vacuuming can restore that cream colour your carpet used to be, it's time to wash it. For this, you will need either a professional or you can, entirely at your own risk, have a go yourself. If you do it yourself, use a commercial carpet cleaner and follow the specific instructions for your carpet. Start by vacuuming the carpet, and then use a carpet brush to work the cleaner in. Allow to absorb, and then vacuum to remove the residue.

....

NB: for a home-made carpet cleaner, try white vinegar and hot water in a 1:10 ratio – but remember to test on an inconspicuous patch of carpet first.

....

Wood/vinyl/tiles/laminate (mopping): vacuuming is not only for carpets – all floors are created equal and all should be vacuumed or swept regularly.

1. Once vacuumed, fill a bucket with hot water and a small amount of detergent or special floor cleaner. (Different surfaces require different products, so make sure you're using the appropriate one.)
2. Dip the mop into the bucket, wring it out (either with the attached lever for flashy mops, or on the inside edge of the bucket for mops more ordinary) and sweep it across the floor. Ideally, this should be done in straight lines for sponge mops, or grand figures of eight for rag mops. However, you won't be expected to pass a breathalyser test or learn advanced ballet, so as long as the mop covers the whole floor at some point, you're doing OK.
3. Rinse and wring out the mop as you go and scrub harder over spots or stains. Once finished, resist the urge to inspect your work in a distant corner or go sock-skating – let the floor dry.

....

NB: before starting, make sure that you place yourself at the side of the room furthest from the door and work towards the door so that you have an easy escape route – one that doesn't involve walking straight across the wet floor, or clambering over precariously balanced pieces of furniture.

....

Warnings:

- **Never wet-mop a wood or laminate floor (that is, use a damp mop but never saturate it).**
- **Avoid harsh detergents.**
- **Don't polish or wax laminate flooring.**
- **Never scour wood or laminate.**

BATHROOM SPECIAL

Having completed the majority of household cleaning tasks, the game is almost won, but a couple of rooms demand special attention: the bathroom and the kitchen.

For many people, bathrooms are the bane of all housekeeping. Unfortunately, they are completely necessary, but regular cleaning is the key to avoiding the worst of the bathroom gremlins. Some people clean their bathrooms every day, and this would certainly be ideal. But the absolute minimum should be once a week as this is the place in the house where germs are most likely to *fester* – ignore at your own risk.

NB: before cleaning the bathroom, open the doors and windows; some of the chemicals used for this kind of cleaning are very strong and should not be inhaled.

1. It's generally best to begin by spraying your bath, shower, sink and toilet with a commercial bathroom

spray. NEVER mix bleach and ammonia as this can be reactive and hazardous; choose one and stick to it.

2. Let this sit for a few minutes, following the specific instructions as to how long, and giving you time, if you're really efficient, to clean the mirror with a bit of polish or glass cleaner, and the surfaces with a general-purpose surface cleaner.

3. Then, using a dry cloth, wipe the solution off. Most of the dirt and scum should come away easily. However, if it doesn't, which is likely if you haven't cleaned the bathroom for a year, try using some mildew or lime-scale remover.

4. Next, wipe the spray away starting at the sink, then from the bath/shower, and finally the toilet, working from the outside in. (The toilet is the place where the worst of the germs will be so you don't want to spread them around by tackling the toilet first and then using the same cloth for the rest of the bathroom.)

5. To finish the toilet, you should then scrunch up your nose in disgust, spray a small amount of bleach around the inside of the toilet bowl, scrub with a toilet brush, and flush.

This is the worst over with. Now, make sure that all surfaces are rinsed with a clean, damp cloth and use some bathroom 'shine' spray or polish to shine the taps. A useful item in cleaning hard-to-reach places such as the underside of taps is an old toothbrush – just make sure you don't put it in the toothbrush holder when finished, or your teeth may get a nasty surprise bleach – this is not the way to achieve that Hollywood smile.

Now, simply mop the floor, put out some clean towels, and stand for a moment to admire the sweet smell of success.

....

NB: remember to sterilise your cloths afterwards, as germs can linger. Boiling hot water will usually suffice.

....

KITCHEN SPECIAL

The kitchen is not usually quite as disgusting as the bathroom to clean, but it has potential. Whereas for some, kitchen counters are wiped down regularly, out-of-date food is promptly thrown away and the washing up is always done immediately, for others, dirty dishes can test one's balancing skills, splattered soup can fester into tufts of fuzz all over the wall, and you might be forgiven for thinking that an alien has taken up residence in your rubbish bin. For those of you who fall into the first group – congratulations, this won't take you long. For the rest of us, roll up your sleeves, switch on the stereo and let's get cleaning.

Tidying up: the first thing to do is deal with the clutter, namely the washing up. Clear all your surfaces and sink, either by washing up, loading the dishwasher, or by putting clean items away (not by hiding everything in the cupboard under the sink).

Dusting: your next task is to dust. Use a damp cloth to dust down all the surfaces in your kitchen. Then, dampen the cloth a little more with hot water (and a small amount of mild soap if necessary) and target any spots of grease/dirt/mould. Remember to MOVE everything. The front of your coffee machine might be sparkling, but if there's a new breed of fungus growing behind it, your kitchen is not clean. And don't forget: this is where you eat. Germs are the enemy!

NB: because the kitchen is home to cooking, smoke and pungent smells, your kitchen curtains will get dirty more often than those in the rest of the house. So, remember that these need cleaning too and should be taken down at regular intervals.

Clean the appliances: it's now time to look to your appliances. First of all, spray oven cleaner into the oven and leave it to sit as per instructions. Your next targets are the refrigerator and the freezer. It's not usually necessary to do a thorough clean of this every week, but try to manage it at least every few months. Start by turning the fridge and freezer off and sorting through all the contents, placing them on the kitchen counter, and throwing away everything that has gone off (brown gunk, white fuzz and a terrible stench are usually signs of this – as are expired sell-by dates.) Now, remove all the shelves and trays, and wash these down, then wipe out the entire inside of the fridge/freezer with hot soapy water, or an antibacterial spray. If you have someone to help you lift – or you have extraordinary super-human strength – move the fridge/freezer and have a quick vacuum/dust/mop behind it. Then replace the clean shelves and all of the food items you want to keep, and turn the fridge/freezer back on – hopefully, having remembered to plug it back in before returning it.

....

NB: this task has to be done with relative speed, so don't take your tea or TV break in the middle of it, as all the food on the kitchen counter will start to go off, and the frozen food will begin to defrost.

....

Go back to the oven and wipe off the oven cleaner, thoroughly. You are now ready to tackle the stove. Take all the knobs, burners and other detachable items off the stove and wash with hot soapy water. Wipe down the remaining parts of the stove, then replace the clean detachables, trying to remember where each part came from.

....

NB: if you have an electric hob – lucky you. Ignore all this and just wipe clean. But if you have a ceramic hob don't use soapy water, use clean water to wipe down and a special hob cleaner.

....

Now wipe down the rest of your appliances: toaster, kettle, blender, microwave (inside and out), and so on, remembering to unplug them all first.

The final stages: breathe – it's all downhill from here: take out the rubbish, wash down all your counter-tops and splash-backs with hot water and mild detergent, or a kitchen-specific antibacterial spray, then wash down the sink (bleaching the drain every once in a while). This is your last wiping task, so take a minute to make sure that all strong chemicals have been rinsed from all kitchen surfaces (these could contaminate your food or harm your hands if you touch them) and then put all your cleaning cloths in the laundry. Wash on a hot cycle, and then tumble dry. This should be done regularly to stop them from harbouring germs.

The finishing line: all that's left to do now is to sweep/vacuum and then mop the floor, put the kettle on, and stand back to admire your work. The only problem, of course, is that as soon as you get hungry, you'll have to christen your clean surfaces, use the sweet-smelling oven, create washing up, and start the whole exhausting process all over again.

LAUNDRY: MAN VERSUS MACHINE

Now that your home is clean and sparkling, it simply wouldn't be right if your clothes stank of sweat and smoke. So, it's time to tackle the laundry.

THE SMELL TEST

Before the washing process can begin there's a delicate process of preparation that needs to be undertaken. The first task is determining exactly what needs to be washed.

There is an age-old myth handed down through generations of misinformed men, that dirty clothes left on the floor for a period of days somehow lose their smell and miraculously clean themselves. This is mere illusion. While leaving clothes to air for a few days – albeit on a dirty floor – may well decrease the smell on first whiff, it is a temporary solution and a dangerous test. Clothes that have once been smelly, lost their smell in this fashion and then worn again, will have their smell reactivated like a slow stink bomb the moment that the wearer starts to sweat. It will then be twice as bad as any normal BO because it's mixing the old with the new, and you will quickly become the butt of all jokes and lose all your friends.

So, to prevent such a disaster occurring: ignore the myth. The only smell test of any virtue is to smell your clothes as you take them off. If they stink – put them in the wash basket. If they, like you, still smell of roses, fold them away and put them back in your cupboard.

Now you're ready to wash.

Whites and colours – a necessary prejudice

It's worth remembering that whites and colours MUST be separated. OK, it takes a couple of extra minutes before the washing process begins, but preparation is the name of the game when it comes to washing. Without a proper match-plan, one stray red item can turn everything else pink. So, sort carefully. But hold on a minute; don't think that just because you've successfully separated your own items, you've scored a home run. What about your opponent's plans (in this case, the opponent being the growling washing machine that always seems to remain one manoeuvre ahead)? Always check inside the machine before you put in your load to make sure that a sneaky red sock – and I don't mean the baseball team – isn't hiding inside, ready to pounce on your favourite white T-shirt and scupper your carefully laid plans.

Darks and lights

Now look at your colours and think 'rainbow'. What! – you thought you were finished separating? Sorry, but there's a whole sea of colours out there, they don't all go together and they don't organise themselves willy-nilly. Red does not go next to blue in any rainbow I've ever seen, so it don't go next to blue in your wash! Colours can 'bleed', especially if they're new. This means that the dye in one item of clothing can leak out of the fabric, and if it's next to anything too different, you're going to end up with a whole lot of dingy, discoloured clothes. So we're separating again. Colours now: darks and lights please.

I see you shaking your head in puzzlement. Have you come across a white T-shirt with a coloured logo? Or is it a pair of pink and navy striped boxers? We have reached the interminable sorting problem: an item is both light and dark, or white and coloured. Breathe. These clothes may be having an identity crisis but you need not. If an item is mainly white, or light, with a bit of dark colour, group it with the lights. Bleeding from such a small colour patch should be minimal, and once you've washed an item lots of times it's less likely to bleed anyway. You can actually test how much something is going to bleed by soaking it in a sinkful of water and then observing the colour the water turns. If it's bled a lot then it's probably a good idea to hand wash it. Otherwise, wash it in the machine with similar colours, or if you're sure that no bleeding will occur you can chuck it in with any colour. But be careful – some items are only ever meant to be washed with LIKE colours (that is, reds and pinks, blues and greens, blacks and browns), even when they've been washed hundreds of times, so remember to check the label, where it will usually tell you if this is the case.

Fabrics – stroke and see
Once you've sorted out your colours, the next thing to consider is your fabrics. Always check the label, but

most clothes, like T-shirts, jeans and sweatshirts, have standard washing instructions and can all be chucked in together (still separating whites and colours of course) on a normal cycle of 40° – but not always. A lot of clothes, especially those made from soft, delicate fabrics such as silk, cashmere, wool and satin have specific washing instructions: cold wash, hand wash, dry-clean only, no dryer. Throwing them in the machine will probably ruin them, and most likely your day, particularly if you were planning to wear that particular black satin top to a party that evening.

So you need to make one more pile: delicates. Treat these however the care label instructs. This is not a time for anarchy.

NB: to hand wash, fill your sink with lukewarm water and a small amount of hand-wash liquid. Soak the item in the foam, rinse in clean lukewarm water and hang to dry – putting it in the dryer will destroy the whole process of having hand washed it in the first place.

WEAPONS

You are finally ready to begin your wash and can load your separated piles into the machine. But don't start the cycle just yet. You still need to add detergent – that's the stuff that actually cleans your clothes. This is usually added either in a separate section of your machine or in a ball that goes in with the clothes, depending on what machine you have and what detergent you choose.

There's no set rule as to which detergent to use – it's personal choice really and smell will probably end up being your main means of decision-making. However, there are some important differences:

Liquid/powder/tablets: no real difference here in terms of effectiveness, but the liquid is probably slightly less messy, while also being a bit more expensive. My personal favourite is those little sachets of liquid that you can just throw in with no mess and no measuring.

NB: some detergents can cause **allergic reactions** on your skin. If this happens, simply switch detergents. Non-biological detergents are generally more skin-friendly than biological ones because they don't contain the strong chemical enzymes that help clean stains, or use hypoallergenic ones which are specially formulated for sensitive skin.

Fabric softener: some detergents have softener included, which eliminates one stage of the washing process, but others come separately and need to be added to your wash, unless you want to end up with scratchy clothes that stick together, or unless you have allergies that might react to the softener. This usually comes in liquid form and can be added in a separate section of your machine. Alternatively, you can leave softening to the drying stage and put a softening sheet in with the clothes in the dryer. Again, this is largely down to personal choice.

Bleach: if you're doing a load of whites (and some of them have become dingy) you may want to add bleach to your wash. This will brighten up the white again, but is a delicate process and should never be added to colour washes – unless you want to get rid of the colour. Some detergents actually have a colour-safe bleaching agent incorporated into them, which you can use for all your clothes. Others also contain bleach, but specify that they should be used for whites only. If these decisions are beginning to seem too overwhelming, simply pick a detergent with a colour-safe bleaching agent and think no more. If you're up for a little more complexity – try out the different combinations and see which you like best.

Stain removers: when clothes are stained and not just smelly, you may need to use a special stain remover in addition to your usual detergent. This should be done before the wash, and generally involves rubbing a small amount of the product directly onto the stain. Follow the specific product instructions.

....

NB: don't use too much detergent or the clothes won't rinse thoroughly. Measure it carefully and only use a full measurement when you have a really heavy load.

....

THE WASH

Loading the machine is fairly self-explanatory: load the clothes into the machine. However, be careful not to overload it, as this will hinder both the washing and drying processes.

Setting the cycle is the next big obstacle. Machines vary so much that it's difficult to give a precise explanation of what you should do, but usually the machine itself will have instructions. Once the wash is finished, remove the clothes promptly (otherwise they could shrink) and hang them to dry. If you have a dryer, transfer the clothes to the dryer, but be careful to check labels, as not all clothes can be tumble dried.

FOLDING

After removing clothes from the dryer, try to avoid the urge to bung them all back in the laundry bag and return to whatever more exciting things lay beyond the world of washing. All you need is a few more minutes, and folding your clothes will go a long way to making them look far more like wearable items and less like a crinkled old rag next time you want to wear them. So, fold, not too tightly, and in whatever manner you prefer, but remember that fold lines will probably slightly effect the way the clothes hang when you wear them, so diagonal ones or fancy origami are probably not the best option. It might be tempting to hang some items such as shirts immediately, thus avoiding the folding stage. This will decrease crinkling, but there is a risk of the shirt moulding to the shape of the hanger and not your shoulders, so it's usually better to fold them first.

IRONING

Boring, tedious, time consuming? Yep, all three. And, unfortunately, there's no way to really spice up this procedure. But for some items – like dress shirts – ironing is a necessity, and since you've come all this way, what's a few minutes more? So, turn up the radio, arm yourself with snacks, and let's get ironing.

For most items, the actual process of ironing is fairly straightforward. Run the iron up and down the item until wrinkles have disappeared. Be sure to smooth out the item first, otherwise you might discover that you're actually ironing wrinkles *in* to your clothes – and these are much more difficult to remove than naturally occurring ones. A good trick is to put the rounded end of the ironing board inside the item. That way the front and back can be separated and ironed without the fear that wrinkles are being ironed into the other side.

For more complicated items like dress shirts, divide and conquer. Collars and cuffs need to be ironed separately and carefully to make sure they end up lying in the right place. The rest of the shirt is much easier. Simply start on one side of the buttons and shift the shirt round until the whole thing has been ironed.

There are of course a few hazards to look out for: 1) read all care labels; 2) make sure the iron is not too hot (the smell of singeing cotton is usually a sign that it is); and 3) NEVER leave the iron face down. Not only will it leave a big brown mark in the shape of an iron on your clothes (or a hole if you leave it long enough), but it also might start a fire, and then you'd have to use a fire extinguisher, maybe call the fire brigade, and even make an insurance claim, which is a whole other chapter.

....

NB: if you want to avoid ironing altogether, buy clothes that are meant to look crinkled. Or alternatively, pay someone else to do them for you – ah, the division of labour, the rise of capitalism and the demise of society!

....

KEEP IT CLEAN

Here are some gentle reminders for pain-free washing:

- Check your pockets before washing clothes. Tissue fluff is a nightmare to remove and money will not survive a wash (nor, for that matter will receipts or driving licences – but that's another story).
- Washing machines may be designed to clean your clothes, but they don't tend to clean themselves, so keep them clean, otherwise your clothes won't be. Dryers have a lint filter, usually found on the door, that collect a whole pile of yuck. This can be easily

cleaned by regularly removing the screen from the filter and simply wiping off the lint.

- If you don't have a washing machine at home and are hauling your dirty clothes off to a self-service launderette, remember that washing machines will need money – usually 20p pieces or £1 coins.
- If you are intending to use such a launderette, be vigilant at watching your machine. Veteran washers have no time for novices and a machine that's finished its cycle will usually be emptied if left unattended. This can often mean finding your lovely clean clothes dumped in a pile of spilled detergent on the floor. Of course, this washers' 'etiquette' means that you are also perfectly entitled to empty out another machine should the need arise – but make sure the cycle is finished, try to give the washer at least a ten-minute grace period, and remember that emptying someone else's wash might mean having to touch their undies.
- Wherever you are doing your laundry, washing takes time, sometimes up to 75 minutes for each cycle, plus drying, so try not to remember suddenly that you need to wash your interview shirt 10 minutes before you need to wear it.

Tips, secret potions and old wives tales

If, even after following all the pearls of wisdom listed above, your home still doesn't feel as clean or sweet-smelling as you'd like, here are a few home-cooked remedies for you to try – follow at your own risk:

- Add a dash of vinegar to warm water to stop streaks forming when cleaning glass.
- Clean grease from wood furniture by immediately adding salt to the stain. Wait until the grease is absorbed, then wipe with a dry cloth.
- To get rid of water marks on wood, spread a couple of tablespoons of mayonnaise onto a paper towel and place it on the water mark. Press lightly then leave for about 15 minutes. Another remedy for water marks is to rub a small amount of toothpaste onto the spot then remove with a damp cloth. Dry and polish.
- To hide scratches in wood, rub the scratch with a piece of oily nutmeat such as pecan or Brazil nut, avoiding the area around the scratch. This will darken the scratch to match the wood.
- Combat old microwave spills by heating a glass of water in the microwave to boiling point. The steam will help loosen the grime, which you should then be able to wipe clean. (If the microwave smells, add a little lemon juice to the boiling water.)

- Get ink out of leather by spraying with hairspray and then wiping with a clean cloth.
- To get grease out of leather, blot the excess then sprinkle the spot with talcum powder. Leave it for at least four hours, then wipe clean.
- To remove chewing gum from all materials, rub the gum with a plastic bag of ice-cubes. This will harden the gum, allowing you to then pull it off in one clump. If any gum remains, heat it with a hairdryer and then rub off with a clean cloth.
- To make a good air-freshener, boil cinnamon and cloves on the hob, then simmer for 30 minutes
- To make a general household cleaner, dissolve a small amount of bicarbonate of soda in warm water.
- To make a good all-purpose surface cleaner, mix equal parts of vinegar and salt to form a paste. Apply with a cloth and then rinse.
- To clean carpets, sprinkle bicarbonate of soda liberally over the entire carpet. Wait at least 15 minutes, and then vacuum.
- To clear blocked drains pour half a cup of salt and half a cup of bicarbonate of soda down the drain. Follow with six cups of boiling water and leave overnight. In the morning, rinse with lots of water.
- Marks from black-soled shoes can be combated with a paste of bicarbonate of soda and water.
- Get rid of smoke from clothes by hanging them over a bath filled with hot water and a cup of vinegar.

- To remove rust from tins, rub with a peeled potato dipped in bicarbonate of soda.
- To get rid of rust on knives and silverware, pierce an onion with the rusty knife, leave it for 24 hours and then remove and rinse.
- For a good homemade furniture polish, mix half a cup of lemon juice with one cup of vegetable oil.
- Add a small amount of fabric softener to your cleaning liquid to pick up pet hair from carpets and furniture.

Admiring your work

Your cleaning is now complete. Your clothes should be clean, your windows sparkling, your bathroom smelling wonderful. This is proof positive that you are, as you had suspected, an absolute cleaning whiz. If, on the other hand, it has not been such a successful venture, take heart. There's such a large community of people just like you out there that whole businesses have been set up to help you out – they're called cleaners and will do all of the above for you. Skip a few meals, save up your coins, and pretend that you just don't have the time to do the cleaning yourself!

5
DECORATING

For some people, decorating is in the blood. While most of us scratch our heads and start ploughing through the Yellow Pages as soon as a room needs work, for these gifted few, a paintbrush, roll of wallpaper and complicated design plan can be produced in two minutes flat.

When my friend Ben moved into his new apartment, he decided that his bedroom needed wallpapering and that he would tackle this task himself. Before we go on, there's something you should know about Ben: he's not a DIY kind of guy. That's not to say he's not macho enough – he plays rugby, swings a pint and burps the national anthem with the best of them. But DIY requires a certain kind of macho: the kind that can measure a wall and handle a paintbrush. And in Ben's case the macho he needed came in the form of his sister Jill. You see, DIY-macho is not gender specific.

The thing was, when Ben went to the DIY shop by himself, he bought paint that *looked* blue, he found a lumpy wallpaper for underneath that was meant to make the paint seem stripy, and he even bought a can of wallpaper paste. But he only bought enough wallpaper to cover half of his room, he forgot the primer altogether, and because he didn't know anything about paint, he couldn't tell the shop assistant if he was looking for matt or gloss, emulsion or solvent, and so picked up the nicest looking can – which turned out to be metallic top coat for a kid's playroom.

Luckily, Ben's sister *did* know about paint, and rescued him from the bombsite that was his bedroom relatively soon after the wet wallpaper (that turned out to be grey) had slid its way down the wall and onto the floor – which he'd forgotten to cover.

But don't despair. Decorating isn't purely genetic and you don't need a DIY super-sister, even if your skills *are* on a par with Ben's. Handling a paintbrush is like riding a bike, so you only have to conquer it once, and even the most inexperienced of decorators can learn to do the basics. It's all a matter of know-how. So here's how:

Planning

MEASURING

The first thing to do when you decide to decorate is to measure the area to be decorated and calculate how much material you will need. This is something that everyone has experience in. Remember all those relentless problems at school? The ones that said, 'If you want to paint a wall with an area of 12 x 12m, and cans of paint cost £1.23 per 1.5m^2, how much will it cost you to buy enough paint for the entire wall?' Well, here at last is the reason for them, but don't worry if your maths is a little rusty, just measure the wall and ask the shop assistant to work out how much paint/wallpaper/plaster/ you will need.

Measuring itself should be simple. You are merely writing down the distance from one side of the wall to the other (remembering to measure in a straight line). However, when I say 'measure' I don't mean get out your 30cm ruler. Buy a proper metal tape measure and write down all the measurements – remembering to factor in the area of windows and doors.

Accurate measuring at the start is essential. You won't be happy if you spend twice the amount necessary and have to return half of the materials, especially if you have to lug it up and down three flights of stairs. And if you end up needing more than you bought, that's an even bigger disaster, as the shop could have run out of the matching colour paint or discontinued the brand of wallpaper – and then you're really stuck. So, get it right at the start.

SHOPPING LIST

The next thing to do is to make a list of everything you need. For wall preparation and painting this includes:

- Bleach
- Brush – stiff bristle
- Brush – painting
- Bucket
- Cloths
- Dust sheets
- Dust mask
- Goggles
- Filler
- Gloves – chemical resistant
- Ladder
- Masking tape
- Paint
- Paint remover (turpentine)
- Paper towels
- Primer
- Putty
- Putty knife
- Roller – painting
- Sand paper
- Scraper – shaped and straight
- Sealer
- Sponge

I'm afraid that we're not going to get more complicated than painting. If you want to do more, then you're obviously far too advanced a decorator to be reading this chapter – or else you need a professional (or a far more expansive decorating book).

So, having made your list, it's time to head to the shop. Once there, you have officially entered the DIY world and, theoretically, any one of the shop assistants should be able to assist you. However, just in case it turns out that they can't, it's a good idea to brush up on your brushes and paints:

TYPES OF PAINT

Paints can be separated into a few general categories according to their base, and also according to their finish:

Base

Water-based *(emulsion)* paints: these are quick drying, don't smell much (so you could even sleep in the room that night), and for those of you who are green-minded, they are also more environmentally friendly. They're used most on interior walls and ceilings.

Solvent based *(oil)* paints: these are slower to dry, more smelly and less environmentally friendly, but they give a very hard, smooth finish and benefit gloss paint because they're more adhesive. They're often used on interior walls and woodwork, but can crack over time.

....

NB: after using solvent-based paints, you need to use white spirit or turpentine to clean your brushes. For emulsion-based paints, soap and water should do.

....

Finish/sheen

Matt: matt paint is good for walls and ceilings that are imperfect (that is, like most of us, have lumps and bumps), because they're non-reflective, and, like any good foundation, disguise flaws. However, they're not so good at deterring future flaws, as they scuff and mark easily. Fortunately, some 'wipeable' matt emulsions are now available.

Silk or satin *(eggshell finish)***:** these are more shiny than matt paints, but not as shiny as glossy ones, which means, they are *quite* good at hiding flaws, *relatively* wipeable, and *fairly* hardwearing. In essence, they're a good compromise.

....

NB: eggshell paints will often contain a fungicide to prevent against mould growth, so are excellent for rooms of high-humidity such as kitchens and bathrooms.

....

Satinwood and semi-gloss: this sheen level is somewhere between eggshell and gloss. So, as you can guess, it's shinier than eggshell and matt, and more hardwearing, but is less good at hiding flaws. For this reason, it's best used on smaller surfaces that need to handle a lot of stress such as skirting boards.

Gloss: this paint is very shiny, hardwearing and smooth. It's easily wiped clean and doesn't mark easily. However, because of its shine, it accentuates flaws in the surface. For this reason, it's best used on small areas such as intricate woodwork.

Getting fancy

Having mastered the general terms, it pays to be as specific as possible when picking your paint to ensure that it most perfectly fits the job at hand. So, for those who think they're hard enough, here's a quick run-down of a few paint particulars:

- **Ceiling paints** need to be thicker than normal emulsion paints to minimise splatter. Rollers are best for application.
- **Textured paints** contain sand or other small particles that make the paint thicker and give it a rough texture. Good for covering cracks and surface flaws. Gives a grainy finish. Best applied with a roller.
- **One-coat paints** give good coverage in just one coat so these are quicker and easier for novices.
- **Children's-room paints** are generally quick-drying emulsion paints that are specially designed to be durable and wipeable. Ranges often include special features such as blackboard paint and glitter glazes.
- **Floor paints** are low sheen with either a water or solvent base. They are tough and hardwearing. Best applied with a roller.
- **Metallic and pearlised paints** do exactly what it says on the tin: give a metallic or pearl look to the finish. Wall must be primed first.
- **Historical paints** such as lime wash. Create an aged effect.

- **Heat-resistant paints** are good for radiators, pipes, and so on (but don't paint when the object is still hot).
- **Masonry paint** is designed for exterior walls because it hides imperfections and repels dirt. It contains fungicide.
- **Metal paint** is different from metallic paint, which gives a metallic look. This is paint for using on metal such as gates and drainpipes. (Make sure the surface is clean before painting.)
- **Waterproof paints** are good for coating exterior surfaces such as guttering or concrete.
- **Wood varnish** is good for shelves, stairs, skirting boards and anything wooden that you don't want to look painted. Like normal paint, this comes in a range of sheens and colours and is generally hard-wearing.

Primers and undercoats

For your basic bedroom revamp, where you're simply changing your wall colour 'cos you feel like a change, primers may not be necessary. However, if your paint or wallpaper is beginning to peel or go patchy, the wall needs to be prepared and primed.

Primers prepare the wall for the paint and are important because they help the paint stick to the surface and prevent any stains from bleeding through. Undercoats are like the first rough layer of paint and are also a good idea, as they have good hiding power and make the topcoat look far smoother – and far more professional. You can generally use the same paint for your undercoat as you've chosen for your topcoat, but you might prefer to opt for a cheaper paint (so long as the colour is similar), as this layer will never really be seen; it's also useful because you can see where you have and haven't painted.

NB: there are different primers for wallpaper and paint, and also for different surfaces, so make sure you pick the appropriate one – it should say what it's for on the can.

PAINTBRUSHES AND ROLLERS

It might seem that paintbrushes are not all that important – I mean, it's the paint that you see, not the brushes, right? Well, yes, but taking the time to select an appropriate brush can make all the difference to the finish. For example, different-sized brushes have different functions: smaller brushes for smaller things like doorframes and trim; larger brushes for large wall areas. But the quality of the brush is harder to spot and can make a real difference too. High quality brushes are structured so that the paint is applied more evenly and efficiently, so the finished job will look far smoother. Look for brushes with long bristles, tapered at the edges, with a divider inside; a wooden handle is also easier to grip. And if you're ready to get ultra-specific, choose a brush with synthetic bristles when using emulsion paint, and natural bristles for solvent-based paint.

....

NB: always prime the brush before you start – with water, for water-based (emulsion) painting, and with white spirit for solvent-based painting.

....

But of course, paintbrushes are not the only option when it comes to painting. Sprayers are available – although probably best left to the advanced decorators. And rollers are a common favourite – probably because they're quicker and much more fun to use. (However, bear in mind that the fun may well have worn off after rolling an entire wall.)

Like paintbrushes, it's worth looking for a quality roller, as it will apply the paint far more smoothly and thickly, drip less, and shed less fibre for you to pick off the wall painstakingly afterwards. It also shouldn't crack halfway through the job and will be reusable, so ,although more expensive at the start, in the long run, you're probably saving yourself money. A general rule of thumb is the thicker and fluffier the roller is, the better. As for the material, rollers follow the same principle as brushes: use synthetic rollers for emulsion paint, and natural rollers for solvent-based paint.

Preparation

Having bought your tools, the next thing to do is prepare the area to be decorated by protecting it. Move as much furniture as you can out of the room and cover any remaining items with dustsheets (old linen or towels will do). Take the curtains down and cover the floor with more sheets or old newspaper. Now look to the surface to be painted.

Walls and ceilings

Your first task is to clean the surface. For walls in really good condition, a quick dust should suffice. However, for most walls, start by checking for fungus – very irritating to remove, but necessary, otherwise it's likely to keep growing, poke its stubborn little head through your new paint job, and ultimately ruin all your hard work. If you spot some, check for a source: is there a water problem, for example? If there is, deal with this first, otherwise the problem will just repeat itself. (It's not enough to be tough on mould, you must be tough on the causes of mould.) Then, treat it with a fungicidal wash, or a home-made mixture of water and bleach (3:1). Sponge the wash onto the affected area and the immediate surrounding area (just in case that stubborn, alien-like creature has begun to spread), leave it for around 20 minutes before reapplying, then rinse it off, wash it thoroughly (using a mild detergent), and rinse again.

Obviously, if there's no mould around you can skip the above step, but most walls will need a bit of filler to smooth out the dents and cracks, and *all* walls should be cleaned before painting. So remove any other surface dirt by scrubbing with water, detergent, and a stiff bristle brush.

For walls that don't need priming, this should be the extent of your preparation. You can now simply wait for the wall to dry completely, then apply your undercoat and paint. However, for walls that do require priming, to give the paint the best finish (or to help the wallpaper go on the most smoothly), they should first be sanded. Glossy surfaces in particular need to be dulled to help the paint stick, and new plasterboard may have joins and patches that need special attention.

To sand, use a fine-grade sander and rub evenly over the surface. Follow with a damp cloth to remove dust. New plasterboard or plaster should then be treated with wall sealer. Allow this to dry and then apply your primer.

you're careful not to gouge or scratch the surface. And wire brushing is another effective and relatively simple technique. Chemical removers can also be used, but these require a touch more expertise, so are perhaps best left for the professionals.

....

Previously wallpapered surfaces need to be treated slightly differently. It's generally advised to remove the old wallpaper before painting or applying new wallpaper, but sometimes, if it's in good condition, it's possible to paint over it. If removing, begin by peeling, soaking and scraping off the wallpaper. Scrub off any glue and wallpaper residue, and then sand and prime as usual. If painting over the wallpaper, make sure any loose wallpaper is properly glued down, then apply a sealer before priming as usual.

Your walls should now be clean, smooth, primed, and ready for painting.

....

WARNING: if your walls contain asbestos, **DO NOT SAND**, as the dust created can be extremely hazardous. If you suspect that your walls might contain asbestos, it's best to consult your local authority before proceeding.

....

Woodwork

All wood must be clean and dry before painting – it should also not be on the point of collapse, so treat any mould as above and fill dents with a fine surface filler or a flexible wood-filler for larger cracks. Wait until this has dried, then lightly sand with fine abrasive paper. Finally, use a wood primer. You are now ready to varnish or paint.

NB: if the wood has been previously painted, you don't need to remove all of the paint, unless it is flaking. Simply clean it, sand it down, apply an undercoat and paint. Remember, however, to wear a mask when sanding as old paints can contain lead, which is hazardous.

Metalwork

Begin by cleaning the metal and removing as much rust as you can with wire wool. Use a rust-killing jelly for the really persistent rust, but be careful as this can burn your skin. Next, treat severe corrosion with a wire brush attached to a power drill. Finally, use a metal primer, making sure to pick an outdoor or indoor one, depending on which is appropriate, and choosing one that is compatible with the metal you are painting.

NB: lead pipework needs only to be rubbed with wire wool dipped in white spirit before painting.

Painting

The first rule of painting is to choose the right conditions for application: when it's neither too hot nor too cold, and in a room that's as well ventilated as possible – perhaps a good time to invest in a fan. By now your room should be fully protected with cloths or newspaper and the surfaces fully prepared and primed, so all you need to focus on is the paint.

Walls and ceilings

Where walls and ceiling are concerned, a good idea before even opening the can is to apply masking tape around the edges of the walls and over the frames and skirting, since most people don't have the precision of a fine-artist. This allows you to paint quickly, without worrying about smudging or dripping over the edge. (The idea is that mistakes will go onto the masking tape, which can then be peeled off at the end to reveal a perfectly smooth line.)

Stir the paint before using it, and then pour into an appropriate container (a small can for small brushes, a roller tray for big brushes and rollers).

The best place to start is the ceiling. Let this dry, then move on to the walls, and, finally, do the more delicate trim. Deal with one surface at a time, finishing an entire area before moving on to the next so that the paint dries evenly. Work from the edges in and try to roll or paint evenly in big strokes, blending overlap marks as you go. Let this dry, then apply a second coat if necessary. To keep trim neat, clean your brushes as soon as they become overfull or messy.

Woodwork

Build up layers. *Always* use a primer, and at least one undercoat and topcoat. Use a small brush and paint in careful cross strokes (horizontal then vertical strokes) for the best finish. Gloss or satin paint is usually most effective on wood.

Metalwork

Satinwood is usually the best type of paint for metal. Make sure the surface is thoroughly prepared and primed, and then apply two to three coats of paint. Pay extra attention to edges, as these are the areas most likely to be brushed or banged against, thus putting a lot of stress on the paint.

Outside

When painting outside, it's particularly important to choose good weather conditions, for obvious reasons. However, be careful not to paint when it is too sunny, as water-based paints will dry too quickly, or when it is too windy, as little bits of your garden, or the rubbish from next door, will get stuck to the paint and ruin your finish. Make sure to use an exterior paint with protection against damp.

Common things to paint

- **Radiators:** make sure to paint them when they're completely cold, using a solvent-based paint suitable for metal.
- **Metal gutters:** coat with a layer of bitumen-based paint to protect against the wet.
- **Windows:** if possible, remove all window accessories (such as the lock) before painting. Wedge the window open as you paint, and try to paint early in the day so that it has as much time as possible to dry before you have to shut the window. (It may get stuck shut if you have to close it when it's not completely dry.) Paint the window from the inside out: starting with the glazing bars and horizontal rails, and finishing with the outside frame.
- **Doors:** remove the handle and other accessories, and wedge the door open. Paint the door, including the top, bottom and hinges, and then the doorframe.

Style and flair

CHOOSING COLOURS

Be aware that the tiny swatch of colour that looks like a gorgeous cornflower blue on the front of the paint can will not always look quite so lovely when covering a 5 x 5m wall. The surface of your wall, the light in your room, and simply the fact that your wall is much bigger than the swatch can make the colour appear altogether different, so it's important to test all colours, on different walls, and in different lights, before you buy the bulk of your paint.

Most paint brands have now made this very easy for you by creating a whole range of small paint samples that you can buy for a pound or two each and take home to test on your wall. This really is a good idea and an important stage in the painting process. Yes, it may delay you for a few hours, but it's worth it to get the colour right. (Just remember to make a note of which colour on the wall corresponds to which sample; if the shades are similar, they can be very easy to confuse.)

Ultimately, which colour you end up choosing is down to personal taste, but remember that you could be stuck with this colour for a long time, so think about the use of the room and how seeing the colour every day will make you feel; the bright red that seemed like a good idea for your sexy boudoir, might not seem so clever when your bedroom becomes the recuperation location for a hangover or a migraine.

Besides, according to many psychologists, colours can have a very strong impact on your mood and emotions, so pick a colour to set the mood:

- **Red** excites the senses (some scientists even claim that it makes our hearts beat faster). It's bold and emotional. Good for a gym, playroom – or bedroom, so long as you have another one in which you can actually sleep!

- **Orange** also excites the senses, but less so. It's cheerful and has been known to increase the appetite. A good choice for a kitchen or dining room, although perhaps not if you're on a diet.
- **Mellow yellow** is all about enlightenment and concentration. It's meant to help speed the metabolism and improve concentration; good for a small dark office, or the kitchen.
- **White and creams** are great for hallways, creating light, striking spaces and as a base to add other accents. White is traditionally associated with purity, simplicity, cleanliness and peace, and is the colour of minimalism. A very modern look; however, be careful of making a room feel too sterile and cold.
- **Green** is the colour of nature. It refreshes the spirit and makes you feel calm and secure. Good for bedrooms, bathrooms and studies.
- **Blue** is overwhelmingly associated with tranquillity. Some research suggests that blue actually causes the body to produce calming chemicals bringing comfort and serenity. A natural choice for bedrooms and bathrooms.
- **Pink** is traditionally considered a colour for sensitivity, femininity and sharing. Good for living rooms and bedrooms (but maybe only if you're a six-year-old girl).

- **Purple** is the colour of royalty. Purple exudes luxury and sensuality and is known to inspire imagination. Good for a bedroom, living room or study.
- **Brown** is the colour of the earth. This symbolises comfort, security and contentment, so it is good for peaceful bedrooms. Also a great neutral colour for communal areas such as living rooms and hallways.
- **Black** means sophistication, elegance, power and style. However, black is also associated with mourning, fear and anger, so make sure you and your room are strong enough for it – or use it as an accent to another colour.

PAINTING TRICKS

Apart from setting the mood, colour tricks can also be used to alter the style of the room cleverly and create an altogether different perspective. For example:

- Architectural features in the wall or ceiling (such as coving) can be accentuated by painting it a different shade or colour.
- Painting one wall a different colour to the rest can create a focal point for the room and can give structured square- or rectangular-shaped rooms more of an interesting character.
- Using the same shade, or slightly different shades of the same colour in different areas can have a unifying effect. For example, carrying the same colour from a

small hallway into the adjoining lounge can make both rooms seem bigger. This trick can also pull together surfaces of different materials such as tiled and painted walls to enhance the perspective of space.

- Dark colours on ceilings will make them appear lower, but can help to minimise exaggerated roof slants.
- Light colours absorb less light so help hide surface irregularities.
- Long, narrow rooms can look wider if you paint the shorter walls a darker colour than the longer walls.

However, there is a warning before you start trying out all of these tricks: make sure that your colours still match the other items that will be in the room.

Begin by considering your major pieces of furniture, such as headboards, cupboards and sofas. You don't have to pick the same colour as these items (and in fact, it's probably best not to, as you'll never find a perfect match), but make sure you choose something that will complement them. So if you have a red couch, don't paint the walls pink, unless you're a punk, a hippie or a member of a boy band. Also, make sure that the colour matches the fabrics in the room such as curtains or bedspreads. And if there's wallpaper to consider, make sure this ties in with the paint – a slightly clashing pillow can be hidden; a whole wall can't.

However, remember that your home is *your* territory and you want it to reflect *you*, so don't pay too much heed to colour charts or friends' suggestions. Choose colours that *you* like, and don't pick for the benefit of fashion or anybody else.

....

NB: if you're decorating a room in order to sell or rent the property, you might not want it to reflect you quite so much. I'm not saying that 'you' isn't great, but 'you' are unlikely to have exactly the same tastes as someone else. It's usually advised to keep the colours neutral (whites and creams) so that the buyer has a blank canvas for their own particular 'you'.

....

You are now officially finished. However, to lay claim to having conquered DIY decoration in the real world, you have to leave the room looking finished too. And I'm afraid that involves cleaning up. Sorry, but I know you know how ('cos there's a whole chapter on it) so take a deep breath, pick up the vacuum, and clean.

Bigger jobs

For bigger jobs (or small ones that you don't want to do yourself), your first port of call will be a decorator or a builder. The best way to find one is through personal recommendations, as this gives you a good chance of finding someone who knows what they're doing and will do it well. Ask your friends if they know anybody good. If they don't, ask for help from local trade bodies.

If this fails, resort to the Yellow Pages and Internet, but be sure to get lots of quotes before you pick one, find out if they're part of a respected trade body, and monitor tea breaks carefully – if more time is spent drinking tea than is spent painting, chances are you're being screwed.

NB: don't forget to ask for references – and check them. This is normal practice in almost any job so if you encounter resistance, it's likely there's a reason why!

It can sometimes be a good idea to arrange to pay for the job as a finished whole, rather than per week, just so there's no incentive for the project to drag on. However, if you do this, make sure the decorator agrees not to take on any other jobs before yours is finished, otherwise you could end up with a half-painted bedroom and a promise that they'll return to finish it by the end of the week, or month, or year.

WARNING: Get everything in writing before work starts. This should include an outline of the work, date of completion, working hours, payment schedule, arrangements for disposal of materials, and so on. Make sure you personally see the decorator/builder's insurance certificate, and be cautious about any 'deals' that are VAT-free; you may need a proof of payment at a later date and the chances are that if he's avoiding VAT, you won't get one.

Whether you hire a decorator or do it all yourself, one final word of decorating advice: be prepared for hassle. Inevitably, things won't always go smoothly – even if the paint does. But just remember, it will all be worth it in the end: you'll have a brand-new room, with a brand-new look, for the brand-new decorating-literate you. And if you don't ... breathe ... I think *Bob the Builder*'s on sometime after lunch.

6
CAR SURVIVAL: MORE THAN A TO B

The day that I passed my driving test (first time, by the way) went down in my personal history as the day I decided that I attracted bad luck. Years later, with the advantage of hindsight, I realised that luck had nothing to do with it. I was merely underprepared for real life on a real road – and no amount of driving lessons were enough to equip me.

You see, having lasted a whole afternoon at school, pent up with the indescribable joy of my new driving status, I decided to get rid of my red learner's plate, get in the car, and take my first drive – solo. I wasn't going anywhere out of the ordinary, I should have known the route, but to my horror there was something about being behind the steering wheel, and not in the passenger seat, that made places look different. And somehow, somewhere, at a roundabout that I still can't identify except in my darkest nightmares, I ended up losing the road I was meant to be on, and finding myself, quite suddenly, on the motorway.

Now, for experienced drivers or non-drivers, this may not seem like such a big deal. But think back if you can to that first nervousness of driving alone when you'd only just learnt how. This was my *first* time out alone, and I'd *never* been on a motorway! It was already dark, I was already panicking, and at that very moment the heavens opened up and decided to plaster my windscreen with monsoon-like rain. Then a light on my dashboard started to flash. But since the cars whizzing past me at the speed of light were taking up most of my concentration I ignored it and carried on.

By now, my windscreen wipers were going frantically, I was straining to read the road signs, other cars were beeping me, and I had slowed to a healthy motorway speed of 20mph in the middle lane. I decided to call my mum (in those days it wasn't illegal). Of course, she told me to get off at the next exit, pull over and figure out where I was. But I didn't realise I had to be in the left lane in order to exit, so I missed the first turning, and before I could get off at the second one, my car started shuddering, then it shuddered a bit more, and then it stopped (luckily, just after I'd managed to manoeuvre into the hard shoulder). 'Right, I'm coming to find you. Put on your hazard lights!' Mum yelled down the phone. And an hour later she found me halfway down the M1. We called the AA. The AA man filled up the petrol (which, embarrassingly, was all that the problem was), and, very slowly, I followed my mum home.

It was bad. However, had I known where I was going, or how to get off a motorway, the whole thing would never have happened. And had I known what the petrol light looked like, the car would never have stopped. You see, dear reader, car survival is all about preparation. So, here's how to be prepared:

Essential substances

Think of your car as a rather large, rather demanding toddler. It needs a lot of care and attention, sometimes it will throw a tantrum, but it's oh so rewarding in the end. And while you can ignore certain demands for a little while (like a polish, or a wax, or 12in rims), there are some substances that it simply cannot do without.

And since your safety is ultimately dependent on its well-being, it's a good idea to suck it up and cater to these ill-timed whims.

PETROL

The first essential substance, and the one you will have to see to most often, is petrol. This may seem obvious, but last year the AA ranked empty fuel tanks in their top 10 causes of call-out, and it's actually pretty easy to forget to fill up the tank. Theoretically, however, your warning light should give you ample warning. So, having noticed the warning light (which usually looks like a mini-petrol pump), all you need to do is fill it up. For many novice drivers, this is the point when you suddenly realise you've never filled up a tank before. And for some reason, people assume that you will automatically know how to do it. OK, it is fairly self-explanatory, but when you're a novice, it's nice to have a little direction.

The first thing to do is work out which side of the car your petrol cap is on and how it opens. You then need to know what kind of petrol your car runs on as you'll usually be presented with a variety of options; the wrong kind will cause your car to stop and could damage the engine. The most common options are: leaded, unleaded and diesel (although leaded is rare these days). If you don't know which petrol to use, your car manual will tell you.

You are now ready to start the pump. However, if you're pressing the button over and over again and no petrol is coming out, you might find that you're at one of the many petrol stations that now make you decide whether you're going to pay at the pump or at the kiosk *before* you start pumping. Supposedly, they have made it 'easier' for us. Actually, for experienced petrol-pumpers, this *is* easier because it allows you to skip the queue at the kiosk and make a quick get-away. But for novices, it only adds to the fluster. Don't panic. Simply press the option you'd prefer (you need a card to pay at the pump) and this should allow the petrol to start pumping. Pick up the petrol nozzle, put the nozzle into the filler hole then squeeze the handle to release the petrol.

Now, simply hold the nozzle steady, either until it clicks (which means it's full) or until you reach the amount you want to spend (the gauge on the petrol pump will tell you). Replace the nozzle, replace the cap, pay, and you're done.

....

NB: if the nozzle clicks when you've hardly started, this doesn't mean it's full, it means you haven't angled the nozzle properly so the petrol isn't going in. Some cars are trickier than others but just calmly try a few angles until you find the one that suits your car. (And if the impatient driver behind you starts beeping, smile sweetly, and carry on unfazed.)

....

OIL, COOLANT, WIPER AND BRAKE FLUID

All of these substances can be conquered simultaneously because they're all essential, and all located in the same place: under the bonnet. As with petrol, warning lights on your dashboard should alert you when these substances need filling. However, unlike the petrol light, these warnings usually mean that you need to fill up immediately. In most cars, they're not just an early warning, they don't mean 'have a check of your oil next time you get a chance', they mean 'your engine has run out of oil, it's possibly about to conk out. STOP NOW and call for help.' To prevent this, check the levels regularly (at least once a month and always before a long journey), and carry a bottle of coolant and a small can of oil in your car, so at least if these lights do go on, you can survive until you reach the next garage.

To check the levels – and to fill them up – the first thing to do is to open the bonnet. This might sound easy, but sometimes the bonnet release is the same colour as the rest of the car interior and can be hard to spot. Usually, it's somewhere near the dashboard and has a symbol of a car on it, but consult your manual if you're in need of help.

Having done this, wedge it open with the metal rod inside the bonnet and locate the relevant compartments. All cars will have a slightly different layout and you should consult your manual if you're unsure which cap is for which substance (oil doesn't make a good wiper fluid, for example). However, generally, the things you should look for are:

- **Oil:** the cap is usually yellow, orange, brightly coloured, or has a symbol of an oil can on it.
- **Coolant:** a relatively large, round cap, on top of an opaque canister, often with a symbol of water on it.
- **Wiper fluid:** a smaller canister, usually with a symbol of a fountain on the cap.
- **Brake fluid:** often has a symbol of a round brake drum on the cap.
- **Power steering fluid:** usually has a symbol of a steering wheel on the cap.

Checking levels

Once you're sure you've located the correct compartment you can check the levels. For water and wiper fluid you can usually see how much there is just by looking. However, for oil and brake fluid, it's just as important not to overfill as it is to stop it getting too low. So, to check the exact level, take out the dipstick, wipe it with a tissue to remove the liquid, put it back in, then take it out again and look at the mark that has been left by the oil/brake fluid. There should be two permanent marks on the dipstick (a maximum and a minimum), and the fluid should always remain between these two. If it's getting low, top it up. But if it's near the top, DON'T overfill it. Always check the oil level after the car has been standing for at least one hour to allow the oil to settle in the sump.

....

NB: oil and water should be checked at least once a month or before a long journey. The other substances can generally be left to servicing (so long as it's regular). However, whilst you should check the levels regularly, if you find that you frequently need to top them up, there's probably something wrong with your car.

....

Having said that, wiper fluid seems to go like wild fire. You'll know you're out when you press your windscreen wiper button, and no liquid comes out. Instead, the wipers will go back and forth on their own, spreading whatever mud, dirty water, or pigeon poop you were trying to remove from your windscreen all over it. This is the time to fill up your wiper fluid, as being able to see out of your windscreen is rather important, really. Fill it with either a commercial wiper fluid or plain water. (Many people add Fairy liquid or a similar household cleaner, but these shouldn't be used as they will make the water bubbly and cause it to congeal.)

Now, simply remember to replace all the caps, close the bonnet, and, essential substances seen to, you're done.

Tyres

Keeping your tyres in good condition and properly inflated is essential for safe driving.

AIR PRESSURE

The first time I filled up my tyres with air, the biggest thing that struck me was not the issue of having to know your correct tyre pressure, nor the part where my hands got filthy – it was the fact that I had to pay for air. For air! Absurd isn't it? But, unfortunately, at many petrol stations (not all, but many) you will be required to pay. So, the first thing to do is get your coinage ready.

Most petrol stations will have an air and water pump somewhere on site. Find this and park your car as close to the pump as possible. Next, don some gloves. You will then need to undo the cap of the small valve on your tyre and attach the air nozzle. However, before you do this, make sure you know what pressure you're aiming for. If you don't know this already, consult your manual. There should be a chart telling you exactly what air pressure is optimum for your tyres and it may vary from front to back. Look at these carefully: too low and your tyres could overheat and burst, but too high and you're more likely to skid. Both will shorten the life of your tyres.

Insert your money, attach the nozzle to the valve and squeeze the handle, watching the air pressure gauge. (The gauge will be either on the nozzle itself, or on the pump it's attached to.) Keep squeezing until your required air pressure has been reached, then replace the valve cap (presuming that you remembered to put it somewhere safe and it hasn't rolled away into oblivion).

....

NB: ideally, check your tyre pressure once a week, but at least once a month and always before a long journey. If you do a lot of travelling, you might want to buy a mobile pressure gauge with a foot pump to top it up ... also doubles as good roadside exercise.

....

Remember to check the pressure of your spare tyre at regular intervals, as well as the ones on your car; otherwise, when you get a flat, you'll have nothing to replace it with.

....

Changing a tyre

Read this section and you'll never be helpless again! Before you begin, it's a good idea to consult your car's handbook to check if there are any unusual specifications. However, most tyre-changes follow the same basic principles:

- Remove all your passengers – it's difficult to lift up a car with three cheering friends sitting in it.
- Get out the jack and the spanner (from your car's tool kit – usually located in the boot of the car).
- Take off the wheel trim.
- Get your spare tyre ready to hand.
- Put the jack in place (consult your manual for the exact location).
- Use the spanner to loosen the wheel nuts.
- Wind the jack up so that the car is raised.
- Finish removing the wheel nuts, and put them somewhere safe.
- Take off the old wheel.
- Put on the new wheel.
- Screw the nuts back in most of the way (with the flat side facing out).
- Let the jack down.
- Tighten the nuts.

If you have done this successfully, congratulations, you are now a fully-fledged mechanical whiz.

NB: lots of modern cars have a spare tyre called a 'space-saver wheel'. These wheels are not meant to be replacements, but merely a temporary fix until you can get to a garage to repair or replace the punctured tyre. They have a maximum speed limit (usually around 50

mph) and a limited lifespan, so drive slowly and don't leave them on for too long.

....

TREAD

The more you drive your car, the more the treads (grip) on your tyres will be worn away. It's all right for them to be slightly worn, but if they get too low, they could exceed the legal limit, and your car could start to skid.

To check the tread, look at the grooves (raised lumps) in the valley of the tyre. These represent the legal minimum for the tread, so if it gets as low as this, it's time for a new tyre.

Battery

Generally speaking, a battery has a life of approximately five years, and getting it checked at each service should be sufficient. However, be aware that if you leave your car without driving it for too long, the battery is likely to go flat. (It's also likely to go flat if you accidentally leave your car lights on, or sit with the heat and radio on but no engine during an all-night stake out – well, you never know.)

If you get a flat battery, it's easiest to call in a professional – in fact, last year the AA reported this as the number-one cause for call-out. However, if you feel confident and have another car with a fully charged battery to hand, connect the two with jump leads and let one battery charge the other.

....

NB: professional help is advised if you're unsure of what you're doing – jump leads placed the wrong way round can cause thousands of pounds worth of damage.

....

Other important checks

LIGHTS

Checking that your lights work correctly is another important test to do regularly. For this, you'll need either an elaborate mirror set-up, or someone to stand outside the car and watch as you switch on each of your lights (including your brake light). If a bulb has gone, get it replaced immediately.

....

NB: if someone starts hooting at you while driving, don't automatically flick the Vs; it might turn out that good Samaritans actually do exist and they're simply trying to tell you that your lights aren't working, or that you haven't switched them on.

....

CAM BELT

The cam belt is what drives the engine and has a life span of anywhere from three to 15 years. You can't really check the cam belt yourself, but it's important to be aware of so that you can at least ask your mechanic to check it for you.

NB: it's also a good thing to check out when you're buying a used car as cam belts are very expensive, so if you're likely to have to replace it, you should factor that into the cost.

Mechanics, garages and servicing

A good mechanic is hard to find, so when you find one that you can trust, stick with him. As with most industries, the best way to find a mechanic is always through personal recommendation. Otherwise, consult your local papers, Yellow Pages or the Internet, and take your chances.

NB: if you don't know or trust your mechanic, it's a good idea to get a second opinion and quote before you have any work done.

The type of garage you choose is really down to personal taste. Local garages tend to give you more personal service and are less likely to try to sell you more than you need (because large dealerships often work on commission), but if you're happy with your dealership, they might be able to source parts quicker and can be just as good.

You need to put your car in for a service at least once a year, or every 6,000 miles, but each car will have individual specifications about how often this is necessary.

....

NB: if your car has a fault you know about, always mention this to your mechanic when you take it in – a regular service may not find it.

....

Breakdown

There are a number of competing breakdown services who will come, like shining white knights, to rescue you from darkest peril should your car breakdown. Membership of one of these organisations is a real bonus for any driver, so take some time to find the best policy for you.

When you breakdown, the first thing to do is to get you and your car out of harm's way.

If you're on a motorway: pull into the hard shoulder, as far away from the main lanes as possible and, carefully, get out of the car, taking any passengers with you. If you have a mobile phone, use it to call your motoring organisation (such as the AA), or the police motorway control centre. If you don't have a mobile phone, walk to the nearest emergency phone. Go back to your car, but don't get in it unless you feel at risk from another person, as your car could be hit. Don't stand in front of the car in case you are hit. If you do get in, sit on the passenger side, with your seatbelt on, and lock your doors. Leave the car when you feel the danger has passed. Always turn your steering wheel so that the wheels face the ditch – if you are hit then, the car at least won't career onto the motorway.

If you're on a smaller road, pull over to the side as far away from traffic as possible, but try to stop in a well-lit area with lots of people. Put on your hazard lights and raise the bonnet. Again, use your mobile phone if you have one, or walk to a pay phone. Stay in your car (unless there's a danger of collision) and NEVER hitch a lift. Then, wait for your rescuer.

....

WARNING: NEVER ignore problems. Cars are not human, they will not miraculously cure themselves, and surviving with a broken gearbox is not the same as coping with a headache. Problems will only get worse, could cause further damage to other parts, and will end up costing you far more the longer you leave them.

....

Cleaning

How many times have you heard the old adage 'Beauty comes from within'? Well, it couldn't be more appropriate than when talking about your car. Just as drinking lots of water is far more beneficial to your skin than applying a spot cream, looking after your car's insides are far more important than the shine on the hood. However, since we've already covered the inner car-care essentials, there's nothing wrong with looking good too. Besides, there is some amount of necessity involved. For example, if your wing-mirrors are dirty, your vision could be restricted, and that's a genuine hazard. So, in the name of safety, folks, here's how to give your car that ultimate shine:

GET ORGANISED

The first thing to do is gather your tools. You will need:

- Bucket
- Two sponges
- Wash and wax soap
- Chamois leather
- Dust cloth
- Water
- Vacuum/dustbuster
- Furniture polish
- Glass cleaner
- Car polish spray

Your next task is to choose a dry day. Now, I know it's Britain and you could well be waiting a while, but trust me, rain mixed with car wax is not a good look.

WORK FROM THE INSIDE OUT

The best place to start is inside. Begin by taking out all of the rubbish – yes, all the old drinks bottles, chewing gum wrappers, pay-and-display tickets, and festering mould have to go. Then vacuum everything: the mats, under the mats, the floors and all of the upholstery. Next, use the furniture polish to wipe down all the leather, dashboard, doors, and anything else that's visible. Last but not least, polish all the interior windows with a dry cloth, using a glass cleaner to remove any stubborn marks.

You can now progress to the outside of the car. Take your wash-and-wax solution (available from most petrol stations), follow the instructions for the amount needed, and, with a sponge, apply the mixture all over the car, including the wheels. Either hose the car down, or use a bucket of fresh water and a clean sponge to rinse it. Repeat until all the soap mixture has gone.

Your car is now ready to be dried – this is the hardest part to do well. A good time-saving tip is to use a squeegee to wipe off the excess water. You should then use your chamois leather to wipe off any water marks, lines or excess dirt that you've missed while washing. Next, take a dry cloth and wipe the wheels. Then use the cloth you used for the interior windows and polish the exterior windows in the same way.

Finally, if you're particularly car-proud, apply a quick wipe-on-wipe-off spray polish and think *Karate Kid*. Wax on, wax off, then step back and admire the shine.

....

NB: this kind of clean should last one to two months (so long as you don't do a huge amount of extreme off-road mud driving). Alternatively, you can take your car

to a car wash or, for ultra-luxury and convenience, get a mobile car cleaner to come to you.

Your car should now be sparkling in the sunlight. However, this does not yet mean that you and your car have successfully 'survived'. In fact, we're just getting started – there's a whole host of nitty-gritty to deal with before the road's clear (excuse the pun).

Documents – DO NOT LOSE

Before you can legally take to the streets, there are a number of legal requirements you have to fulfil. For example, your car must be registered with the DVLA (Driver and Vehicle Licensing Agency), have a valid tax disc, be insured, hold a current MOT if it is over three years old, and you must have a valid driving licence. Basically, it's time for the paperwork:

DRIVING LICENCE

Before you can even think about driving, even if you have a brand spanking-new car sitting in the driveway, you need to obtain a provisional licence – you can't take your test or even start lessons without one.

Provisional licence

So, fill in the relevant licence application form – available from your local Post Office or from the DVLA – send it off with your passport and a stunning passport-sized photo, and, within a matter of weeks, your ticket to freedom should be in your hands. (Bear in mind when taking your photo that it should be against a plain light background, face on, with no headgear; the DVLA can be very finicky – a slight turn to the left and you could be mistaken for a whole other person, they think.)

....

NB: some Post Offices offer a Premium Checking Service where they will check your passport and validate your application without you having to send your passport away (a good idea bearing in mind the reliability of British post).

....

Full licence

Once you've passed your test, you need to apply for a full driving licence. Officially, you have two years in which to do this, but try to do it as soon as possible because, after a couple of months, it's sure to slip your mind, and if the two years run out, you'll have to take your theory and practical tests all over again (… and by then you will have developed bad driving habits so it will be 10 times harder). Simply complete the declaration on your test pass certificate, complete another licence application form, and send them both with your provisional licence and the appropriate fee to the DVLA. (Yes, of course there's a fee. As you will see, there is a multitude of ways in which money is extracted from motorists. This is the first, but by no means the last – get used to it.)

Loss/detail change

If ever you change your name or address, you're required to inform the DVLA and officially change this on your car documents.

So, to change your **address**, complete the appropriate section of the paper counterpart to your licence, and send it with your **photocard** to the DVLA. If you're changing your **name**, you'll have to fill out a new licence application form, and include proof of your name change as well (such as a marriage certificate). Usually, you'll be asked to provide *original* documents. However, in most cases you can use the Post Office Premium Checking Service to avoid letting them out of your possession, or if you do send them off, remember to make photocopies for your reference in case for some reason they never return.

....

NB: if you have an old-style paper driving licence, get with the times. The DVLA don't issue this kind any more so you'll have to change it to a new photo-card licence when altering any of your personal details. You therefore need to include a photo and proof of your identity (UK passport), as well as the other information above.

....

If you need a new licence for any other reason (such as it's been lost, defaced by an overzealous drunk friend, or stolen, or if you just *really* hate your picture), simply fill in a new licence application form, and apply as above. There will, however, be a fee for replacement.

CAR REGISTRATION DOCUMENT (V5 FORM)

The V5 form specifies the registered 'keeper' of the vehicle. This isn't necessarily the person who owns it, but the person who 'keeps' it (that is, the person who is responsible for it) and the V5 shows their name and address, the registration mark and other information about the car. It's absolutely essential when buying or selling. (Note: the following section has lots of technical info, but bear with it – it's important.)

Buying

You should NEVER buy a car that doesn't have a V5 form, as this is a good indication that it could be stolen. If you buy a brand new car, in most cases, the dealer will register it for you, but if you buy a used car, you must inform the DVLA. Although the onus here actually lies with the seller, as the buyer you also have a responsibility to let the DVLA know about the change and to make sure that you hold the relevant documentation. The relevant documents are:

- If the seller has a two-part registration document, he should fill in the bottom section and give you the top half.
- If he has a three-part registration document, you must both sign the blue section and you should be given the green section of the document.
- If he has a registration certificate, he must fill it in, you must both sign the appropriate sections, and he should give you the green section.
- In all cases, the dealer should then complete the section on the back of the document and send it to the DVLA. Make sure that you always receive one of these documents as they're your proof of ownership and are needed when you apply for a tax disc, insurance, and so on.

NB: if you do buy a car without a V5 (despite my warnings!) you can apply for a new one by filling out a replacement application form (available from the Post Office or the DVLA).

WARNINGS:
- NEVER buy a car without a registration document or certificate.
- If presented with a registration document, use your X-ray vision to make sure it's valid: that is, hold it up to the light (the DVLA watermark should be within the layers of the paper, not merely printed on the surface).
- A registration document isn't necessarily proof of

ownership. You can check the legal ownership by asking VOSA (Vehicle and Operator Services Agency) for a VIC (Vehicle Identity Check).

- The VIN (Vehicle Identification Number) on the car must match the number of the registration document and hasn't been tampered with – scratch marks are not a good sign. The 17-digit VIN on the car can usually be found under the bonnet, or in the floor panel on the driver's side.
- The engine number should match the one on the document.
- Consider having the car checked by an independent qualified examiner.
- You can check the date of registration, year of manufacture, engine capacity, and car colour through the DVLA's checking service.
- Never pay cash – you may need a record of the transaction if it all goes horribly wrong.

....

Selling

If you are the seller, you have all the responsibility. You must give the V5 form to the new owner and it's up to you to inform the DVLA of the change. Here's how:

- If you have a two-part registration document, you must complete the lower section (entitled 'notification of sale and transfer') and send it to the DVLA.

You should then give the buyer the top part and a new registration certificate will be processed.

- If you have a three-part document, you must complete the blue section, both you and the buyer must sign it, and you must send it to the DVLA. You should then give the buyer the green section.

- If you have a registration certificate, you must complete the relevant section, both you and the buyer must sign it, and you must then send it to the DVLA. You should then give the buyer the green section.

- If you sell your car to a trader, you must complete an extra section (depending on your document type) obtain the details and signature of the trader, and send this information to the DVLA.

WARNINGS:

- **Keep a note of the buyer's name and address.**
- **Keep a note of the car's mileage on sale.**

Old cars

Some old cars aren't registered with the DVLA because they missed the computerisation deadline in 1983. You can register them now, by completing the relevant form – available from the DVLA.

Imported cars

Cars imported into the UK must be registered before they're used on public roads. So, however tempting it is to jump into your flashy new import and rev up the engine, you must register it first. Fortunately, registration should take only 2–3 days through your local DVLA.

....

NB: new imported cars can only be registered as 'new' if registered within 14 days of delivery and only if they show 'reasonable' delivery mileage (that is, it doesn't look like you've been zooming around for miles first). Usually, you'll also have to present evidence of 'type-approval' from the supplier or manufacturer, or, if it hasn't been type-approved, it must pass a SVA (Single Vehicle Approval) test. This is an inspection scheme for vehicles that haven't been type-approved to British or European standards to ensure that safety standards have been met before they appear on public roads.

....

To register, the first thing to do is get an 'import pack' from the DVLA and fill out either the enclosed form for new vehicles, or the form for used imports. You then need to send this to the DVLA, including also: the appropriate fee for your vehicle; your British insurance certificate; the car's foreign registration document; evidence showing the date the car was collected; evidence of type approval; the Customs and Excise form; a British

MOT (if the car is over three years old) or a Declaration of Newness; and evidence of your name and address.

....

NB: you may need to consult Customs and Excise to find out what form you need for your particular import.

....

MOT

All vehicles over the age of three years need to have an MOT (Ministry of Transport) test once a year. The MOT certificate proves that your vehicle is roadworthy (in other words, it shouldn't spontaneously combust) and it's necessary before you can get a tax disc, and before your car's allowed on the road. An MOT can be carried out (often while you wait) in VOSA-approved garages all over the country – make sure that your garage is VOSA approved, otherwise the MOT will not be valid.

If you lose your certificate, you should be able to get a duplicate from the garage where your car was tested. However, if the test station has moved or closed, you should contact VOSA direct.

TAX DISC

Before you can drive your car on the road (or even just park it on the road), you must have an up-to-date tax disc. Many drivers try to dodge this and, until recently, a lot of them got away with it because the car had to be physically spotted on the road without tax before a fine could be imposed. Now, however, the government has got clever. All cars that don't renew their tax disc within a month of the old one running out, are now identified in the DVLA computer database and drivers are automatically sent a penalty which goes up if the car remains untaxed – very Big Brother. Tax is an annoying cost, but fines go on top of this and can rise vastly if not paid promptly, so it's better just to pay the damn tax at the start.

....

NB: even if your car's off the road, you're still liable for tax – and still liable for the penalty – unless you inform the DVLA and fill out a SORN (Statutory Off Road Notification) declaration. This is also another reason to inform the DVLA when you sell your car – if you don't it's you who'll be liable for the tax and the penalty, not the new owner.

....

To get a tax disc, take to the Post Office: the tax renewal form (which should be automatically sent to you by the DVLA), or a tax application form if it's the first time you're taxing the car (available from the Post Office); a valid MOT certificate; proof of your car insurance; your car registration (V5) form; and your driving licence. Make sure that all of these documents are in your name, or if they're not (for example, if the car's owned by a company) that you have a letter from the named person/company confirming that the car is for your use.

INSURANCE

So, you know those irritating adverts that appear on your

TV every two minutes? The ones with dancing elephants or people in suits smiling and trying to look sincere? Well, they're adverts for car insurance, and, unfortunately, if you're a driver, it's not a subject you can ignore, although you can at least ignore the adverts by changing the channel.

Car insurance is a legal requirement in the UK so you can't drive a car without it. It can range in price and comes in three basic types:

- **Third Party Only (aka Act Only):** this is the absolute minimum legal requirement and covers third-party liability risk (the damage you may do to others – not to yourself or your car) on public roads only. It's rare to take out this kind of insurance as coverage is poor – you won't get jack if you crash.
- **Third Party, Fire and Theft:** this is the same as third-party insurance, except that it also covers your car for fire and theft.
- **Comprehensive Cover:** gives you 'all risks' cover for your car, so, as with third party, you can claim for all damage you may cause to another car/person, but you can also claim for any damage to yourself or your car. There will, however, be some exceptions in the fine print of each policy.

You can search for car insurance in the newspapers, Yellow Pages, and on the Internet; a number of websites will actually help you find and compare different policies and make direct comparisons. Just make sure you get plenty of quotes before you choose.

Having decided on a policy, the most important thing to be aware of is your **insurance certificate**. You are not legally insured until you have actually received it, or at least a **cover note** and to drive without one is a criminal offence. You'll also need it if you ever make a claim, and every time you apply for a tax disc, resident's permit, and so on. So put it somewhere safe … and try to remember where that somewhere safe is.

....

NB: an insurance certificate should specify the name of the policyholder, the registration number of the vehicle, the date the cover begins and expires, the limitations of use, and the names of the person/people entitled to drive the vehicle.

....

Accidents

If you have an accident, DON'T panic, don't drive off, and don't start crying; actually, if it's your fault, maybe do start crying and get the other person to feel so sorry for you that they tell you not to worry about it, it wasn't your fault, and they'll cover all the damage.

Seriously though, staying calm can be very difficult when you've just been slammed into, and it's difficult to remember all the things you're meant to do. So, a quick checklist:

- If there are any injured parties, call the police and ambulance immediately. If no one is injured, you should still inform the police, if only to get an incident number to help later with insurance claims. However, this can be done with less urgency.
- Never admit liability, even if you know that you were to blame – your insurance company might not interpret it that way.
- Never drive off.
- Don't move your cars until you've noted their position or, preferably, a non-biased witness has noted their position. (However, if you're causing a pile up behind you, it's probably a good idea to move them as soon as you can.) Take a photo of the accident and road if you have a camera with you.
- Exchange personal details (name, number, address) and insurance details with the other driver (then take down their number plate and car details in case they've been lying about all of the above).
- Take down personal details of all witnesses.
- As soon as you can, write down a detailed account of what happened, including a diagram.
- Tell your insurance company.

MAKING A CLAIM

If you have an accident that involves no third party (lampposts don't count) and you need to make an insurance claim, the first thing to do is call your insurance company as you'll need to have your quote for repair approved by your insurer *before* any repair work can be carried out. (If, however, you have comprehensive cover, you should be able to take your car to your insurer's nearest approved repairer immediately, which will have automatic authorisation to repair your car straight away – you won't need to worry about calling your insurer until you're safely home.) Your insurer will then deal with the claim from there.

If you have an accident that does involve a third party (passenger, other driver, pedestrian, cyclist) you need to inform your insurer, who will send you an accident report form to fill in. The third party will be given the same kind of form from their insurer, as at this point both companies will be attempting to work out who is at fault. An outside investigator may also be brought in to look at the accident scene and you may be questioned by both your insurer and this investigator; bear in mind that this could end up in court, at which point lying will a serious offence, so try to get it straight from the start.

Once your insurance company has decided who they believe was at fault (hopefully, not you), they will proceed accordingly. However, there's not always agreement over who is to blame. (Obviously, *we* know it couldn't have been you, but others may need convincing.) When this is the case, a dispute will take place between your insurer and the insurer of the third party, and, ultimately, it could end up in court.

The most important point here is communication. Make sure that you understand what your insurer needs from you, and find out from them what repair work you can go ahead with and when. Remember that you will have to pay the excess (specified in your policy) even if your insurer is paying the repair costs. So, if the repair (or replacement in the case of theft) is lower than the excess, you will not be able to make a claim.

NB: if you have third-party only insurance, and you're in an accident that wasn't your fault (great – now I'm starting to sound like those adverts), you won't be covered by your own insurance, but will need to claim from the third party.

Travel abroad

All UK car insurance policies provide at least minimum cover for driving in Europe. However, it's a good idea to speak to your insurer before you travel to make sure that you have the right cover – the minimum cover might not be the right one.

Resident's parking

So, you've now paid car tax, MOT, car insurance, VAT, council tax – you'd think you'd be able to park your car outside your home, right? Wrong. Being a resident of an area merely earns you the privilege to pay to park in that area.

To get a resident's permit you must obtain the relevant form from your local council, then send this to them, together with your driving licence, proof of residence (such as your council tax bill or tenancy agreement), car insurance document and V5 form. Alternatively, you can take all of this into your local authority's transport office and they should be able to give you your permit on the spot; if, of course, you are prepared to stand on that spot queuing for most of the day.

Penalty points and legal loopholes

As soon as you become a driver it seems that the police take on a whole new persona. Instead of being that bastion of society, that team of crime-fighting heroes, and that nice bobby who your mum told you to find if ever you got lost, the police suddenly become your archenemy – the force standing between you and the open road. It's not that you've suddenly become a criminal, or even that you want to speed down the motorway at 100 mph, but being a driver gives you far more opportunity to do something illegal unintentionally – and unintentionally going a few mph over the speed limit, even in the dead of night, is one of them. So, through no fault of your own, you instantly become Jerry and the police are forever Tom.

However, the thing that gets most drivers is that it doesn't always seem fair, because, unlike a policeman, the cameras are indiscriminate. So, the best way to avoid penalties is to know the rules:

Points ... you do not want these

- Six points in your first two years of driving after passing your test will lose you your licence and you will have to take your test again.
- Twelve points on your licence will force you to go to court with the possibility of being disqualified from driving for a certain amount of time and possibly having to take your test again.
- 'Totting up' 12 points in a three-year period will cause you to lose your licence automatically for a minimum period of six months or longer.
- Points remain on your licence for four years.
- Driving offences (such as drink-driving) can remain on your licence for up to 11 years.

WARNING: Drink-driving and drug-driving are two of the biggest causes of road accidents. Alcohol and drugs alter your perception and your reactions, making you a completely unfit driver. Saying no to a pint in the pub won't make you a social outcast – killing someone will.

SPEEDING TICKETS

Before we begin, it's important to note that speeding is dangerous. Full stop. It is a major cause of road accidents and I am not condoning it. However, it's easy for even the most cautious drivers to slightly exceed the speed limit, and if you do and get a ticket, it's automatically three points and a fine. Of course, if you get stopped by the police and if you've got the gift of the gab, there's always the possibility of talking your way out of it – after all, they're only human (or so they say). So, no matter how angry you are, try not to be aggressive. Yes, they may be power-tripping, but sweet talking and saying sorry is definitely a more effective approach than belligerence. Try to think of it as winning yourself an Oscar, rather than losing your dignity.

There are, however, a few specifics that you can look out for. For example, did you know that if the policeman hasn't checked his speedometer that day, he can't legally issue you a ticket? Ask him when it was last calibrated. (Only traffic police have regularly calibrated and certified speedometers, so it's likely he won't have done this.) Ask to see it. Ask him to prove it's calibrated. Make a note of the speed it says and its serial number. In fact, make notes of everything: what he asks you, your answers, his name, number, car reg., the time, date, position of your car, and so on. This will probably annoy the policeman, but he'll be making notes about you, so scribble away.

NB: if you don't think you're going to get out of the ticket on the spot and plan to fight it in court, **NEVER** admit that you were speeding – it will be used later against you.

Unfortunately, if you get caught by a camera the human factor is lost and the ticket will be automatic. However, it must be issued within 14 days, or they don't have a case, and you should ALWAYS write a letter asking to see photo evidence. If they can't provide evidence (and often they won't) then they have no right to prosecute you – it's against your human rights. If, however, a photo of you grinning behind the dashboard does arrive, write a letter explaining the circumstances and appeal to their better nature – yep, I know it doesn't seem like they have a better nature, but it's worth a go, and at least you're making them work for it.

If speed cameras keep catching you, there exist a range of radars you can attach to your dashboard to warn you as you're driving. Some of the most popular versions are the Road Angel and the Snooper. You might also want to consider slowing down.

PARKING TICKETS

No points are allocated for parking tickets, but they carry an annoyingly high fine (variable depending on the location), and clamping is even more irritating. As with speeding tickets, ALWAYS make notes of everything and always complain if you have good reason.

....

NB: be alert for cowboy clampers. Get all of their details and check with your local authority to see if they're genuine before you pay.

....

Finally, drive carefully. However annoying, it's good to have a reminder that limits exist, because even when you've done everything correctly (got the paperwork in check, a shine on your hood, petrol in the tank and a clean licence) things can still go wrong (a flat tyre, a crash with a lamppost etc. ...). So, don't get too cocky. Besides, even if you're the best driver in the world (and I'm sure you are) no matter what you do, you can never control the driving of others – having said that, you could always buy them this book.

7

THE WORLD OF WORK

Leaving school or university and starting work is akin to being woken up at the crack of dawn with a bucket of ice-cold water and a hangover. It's a shock, and it hurts, and afterwards there's no way you can go back to sleep. Childhood is gone forever. That's the end of Peter Pan.

But there are advantages too: you earn money, you sound grown-up when you introduce yourself at parties, and, if you're really lucky, you get a warm glow of happiness and fulfilment in the knowledge that you are truly making a difference to the world. Of course, this isn't always enough to override the early mornings, late hours and sacrifice of your whole life to 'the man', but you can't remain a student forever. And actually, learning *how* to get a job could almost comprise a university degree in itself.

The first real job I ever had was working for a stereotypically gay Hollywood movie producer who hired me to interview celebrities – sounds glamorous, right? Well, yes, it would have been had I actually done any of the things I very naively believed I was going to do. As it happened, I became a slave to a man who kept me in the office (a conference room in the swanky hotel he was staying in) until 10 o'clock each night, I was regularly woken up at three in the morning with demands to 'fax something real quick to LA', was praised and screamed at with such schizophrenic speed that I felt like my nerves had literally been snatched from my body, and for six weeks was told that the cheque for my services was in the post. I finished the summer with minus money (having failed to receive a penny from him but spent hundreds of pounds on travel cards and his lunch), a nervous rash, an irrational hatred for Hollywood producers ... and a very valuable lesson.

It taught me to get everything in writing, to get contracts signed *before* starting work, to NEVER carry on working without being paid, to be sceptical about big promises, to stand up for myself (especially when told I needed to dump my boyfriend and get a nose job), to keep records of everything – and to know when to quit. That summer I learnt exactly where to draw the line between work-experience and slavery, and was a hundred times savvier when applying for my next job.

But even without such drama, starting work is a dangerous time because you don't know quite what's expected of you, what's normal, what you have to put up with, and what you don't. Fortunately, this chapter will help you find out.

Finding a job

Some people spend their whole childhoods meticulously planning the rest of their lives. By the time they hit the real world, they have a great CV, a long list of work-experience, a job and a plan. Others of us finish school, finish university, kill a bit more time with a masters and a gap year, and find ourselves still wondering, still trying to decide what is the perfect career for us. Stop. Trying to work out what you're going to do for the rest of your life is the surest way to go about doing nothing. It's paralysing. The question is too big. Instead, think about what you might not mind doing right now, and what options you want to leave open for yourself. People don't generally stay in the same firm for their whole lives anymore, or even in the same career, so what you do straight out of university doesn't have to determine your whole life. But get out there. Have a go. Suck it and see.

NB: if you're aged between 16 and 24, not in full-time education, and you don't know what direction you want to take your career, or if you want further qualifications, consider a government Apprentice Scheme. They have flexible time periods, you get qualifications at the end, and receive a training wage while you're learning.

There are five main approaches to finding a job:

1 ADVERTISING

Look through all the papers, journals and websites that list job vacancies, see what's out there, and apply. If you're looking for a local job, look in a local paper. If you want to go into flower-arranging, check the flower magazines. Some papers will advertise different types of jobs on different days, so make sure you look on more than one day, and keep searching. The Internet is a particularly good place to look because it allows you to be specific about your search and has a huge database. You can even sign up to various web-directories, where you fill in information about what kind of job you're interested in, and are then e-mailed matching job vacancies that come up.

2 DIRECT APPROACH

If you already know what kind of job you're looking for, you can go directly to the companies in that field and see what vacancies they have. For example, if you want to go into banking, go to the websites for all the banks and see if they're advertising. Or call them up and ask. Often companies will have periods of large intake when they're actively seeking to employ new people, or they might have graduate schemes set up that take on a certain number each year. This is a great opportunity, as, although there will probably be lots of competition, you at least know that they need new people, so why shouldn't it be you? Just make sure you follow their guidelines about how to apply, and don't miss the boat, as these intakes could be infrequent.

3 SPECULATIVE APPROACH

You can also apply directly to companies speculatively. This involves you offering your services, even when no job is advertised. Your chances of success here are considerably reduced as they will not have planned to take on anyone new, and genuinely might not be able to do so if it's not in their budget. However, if you're particularly brilliant (and I'm sure you are), and you can pick out reasons why you are specially suited to the company, you never know. Plus, there's always the chance that your CV will arrive just at the point that they decide they do need to hire someone. Timing is everything. If you can get in there before the job is advertised to the masses, you have a huge advantage and they might decide to look no further than you. Remember, though, to find out the name of the person you should be contacting – and spell it correctly.

4 JOB CENTRE/RECRUITMENT AGENCY

Both of these services will work on your behalf to find you a job. Registering with them is free, so it's a good idea to join as many as possible to increase your chances of success. Generally, they will begin by interviewing you, testing your skills and finding out about your interests and experience. Many of them will also offer some consultation and advice to help you work out exactly what you're looking for.

The big benefit is that companies with job vacancies actually go directly to them and ask them to find suitable candidates (who ever said a job won't come to you?). So, if you're considered a good match, you'll be sent for interview, and hopefully secure the job. If you don't get the job, you stay on the agency's books and wait to be matched up again.

....

NB: Job centres generally deal with local or temporary work, whereas recruitment agencies will deal with bigger companies, higher-level jobs and candidates looking to start a career.

....

5 NETWORKING

As much as we hate to do it, networking can be vital. It's the old 'it's not what you know but who you know' adage in action. (Now, before you freak out and start blaming your joblessness on your parent's lack of consideration in not being mates with a particular MD, remember: you don't need to know people in high places to network, although this never hurts.) Often, people you know through your own day-to-day contacts will be able to recommend you to an employer, or give you an inside track to a job. So tell everyone you know – the butcher, the baker and the candlestick maker – that you're looking for work, you never know who might come through for you.

And don't feel bad about doing this. You still have to secure and keep the job on your own merits (you won't stay employed for long, no matter how good friends your dad is with the manager, if you seriously screw up) but everyone uses contacts if they can. So *talk* to people. Call in favours. Don't be afraid to ask for help.

Curriculum vitae

When you apply for a job, you will almost always be asked to send a CV. This is the document employers will consider most and is your chance to present yourself in the very best light possible. So, don't be modest and don't hold back: you have sell yourself, baby!

NB: enhance the truth, yes, but DON'T LIE. Making your summer job filing sound slightly more administrative is one thing, pretending you've had 10 years' experience in balancing accounts is another. Even if they don't catch you out in the interview, you will almost always get discovered in the end, and lying on your CV is a sackable offence.

Your CV should be brief (maximum two pages of A4). It should include all your academic and professional qualifications, relevant work experience, IT and other skills, achievements and interests. It should also include your contact details (there's no point in having a glowing CV if the employer doesn't know how to contact you) and your references (a previous employer is best, but a teacher or respected member of society who knows you will do, so long as it's not your brother or Auntie Jill). Lastly, it should be clear, typed and well-presented. Think about what elements make you look best and put them at the start. For example, if you got straight As throughout school, put that in bold on the first page. If you got Ds, but spent every weekend working with underprivileged kids, hide the education section near the end and start with your experience and people skills. And remember, the employer doesn't possess a crystal ball, this piece of paper is the only information they have about you, so tailor each one to fit the job you're applying for, and make sure it shows them just how wonderful you really are.

....

NB: make sure that whoever you put down as a reference will say good things about you. If you've had only one previous employer, you might not have much choice, as this is the person the interviewer will be most keen to speak to, apart from academic references. However, if you know the report won't be glowing, certainly don't volunteer them.

....

Covering letter

Along with your CV you will usually have to send a covering letter. This shouldn't be a stumbling block, and you don't need Shakespearian flair to write a good one. In essence, it's merely a means of introduction and should be very brief (a couple of paragraphs), stating who you are, what position you're applying for (with any reference number) and why, including your best selling point if you have one. (For instance, if the job is for a French interpreter and you lived half your life in France – now is a good time to tell the employer.)

Beyond this basic information, the letter is a chance for you to show how professional you are by laying out a neat, typed and well-presented letter, addressed to the right person (phone and check if you're not sure), and making sure to check for spellings, especially their name (there's no excuse now that computers will check spellings for you).

Interview

Once your glowing CV and letter secures you an interview, perhaps the most important thing to do is buy a suit. It doesn't have to be expensive and you need only one, but it's essential that when you turn up for interview, you look neat, smart and serious about your career. A suit says that you care and will put the employer in a completely different frame of mind when interviewing you than if you turn up in last night's crumpled shirt and a pair of jeans.

The interview itself may be very grilling if they're trying to test your competency in certain areas, or very informal if they just want to find out a bit about you. Try to respond appropriately, but even if you feel very relaxed, never let your guard down entirely, or else you might find yourself letting on that your summer of being an 'editorial assistant' at the local paper, really amounted to you opening the post.

Prepare in advance. You can work out what kind of questions they're likely to ask you (why do you want the job, what makes you qualified for it, what are your strengths and weaknesses, and so on) so don't make things more difficult by having to think of answers on the spot. Inevitably there will be some questions that catch you out, but think carefully about these basic ones beforehand and work out answers that will portray you in the best light.

Have a few questions prepared to ask them. They will almost always ask you if you have any questions, and having some makes you look good. They can be about anything – the job, the company or the structure of the work – and don't forget: they're trying to sell their company to you too. I know, when unemployed, and after doing years of work experience for free, it's tempting to take any job that's offered and be amazed and thrilled that someone should actually want to pay you for your work. But now is the time for your poker face. Of course you want the job, but bluff just a little. Besides, it really is worth taking the time to make sure it's the right job for you. After all, leaving a job after a month doesn't look great on the old CV, so you're probably going to have to stick it out at this place for a little while at least.

Other than that, simply try to be yourself. Be enthusiastic, confident and polite, but don't try to act like someone you're not – otherwise, if you get the job, you might have to enrol in some serious acting classes.

The offer

When your job offer arrives (the power of positive thought is amazing), it's time to celebrate! You have successfully completed your first mission in the working world. But don't go too mad, there are a few more obstacles to think about yet. For example, if the offer's been made via phone or in person, remember to get it in writing.

NB: if they ring you, don't feel you have to give an answer straight away – you are allowed to think about it overnight.

Most employers will give you a standard contract to sign, but don't worry if they don't. It doesn't have to be a 10-page legal document, but it does have to lay out the terms of your employment such as your working hours, job description, notice period (should you decide to leave or they decide to fire you), holiday time and your pay. And it should be signed by the time you start work, or at least within the first couple of weeks. (Legally, a statement of the particulars of your job MUST be given to you if requested, so long as your term of employment is longer than one month.)

NB: most job offers will be subject to references, and employers will almost always check them, so NEVER LIE; getting your mate to pretend to be an MD is definitely a sackable offence.

Also, be aware that you probably won't get paid until a month into the job, so it might not be a bad idea to keep the champagne on ice for a little while longer. Besides, you need to be thinking clearly if you're going to manoeuvre around all the new issues that will be thrown your way.

Your first day

Accept from the start that it's likely to be bad. If it's not, you're one of the lucky few. On your first day, you won't know anyone, you won't know what you're meant to be doing, how anything works or where anything goes. You probably won't even know where to go for lunch. Don't worry. This is normal. It will take you at least a few weeks to feel settled and possibly months to get on top of the job, so don't run screaming after one day. Smile at everyone, be confident, be friendly – and be strong.

P45 form

The first task you will be set on starting your job is presenting your P45 form. 'This is a tax document issued by the Inland Revenue, listing your personal details, your employment start and finish dates, your pay, tax, tax code and PAYE reference number.

If you're one of those incredibly organised people and have your P45 efficiently stored away somewhere, congratulations, simply present it to your new employer and they will update it for you. Alternatively, if you've never had a job before, and don't have a clue what a P45 form is, don't worry. Tell your employer, or the recruitment agency, and they will arrange it for you. If, on the other hand, you *have* had a P45 before but have lost it, you will need to contact the Inland Revenue yourself.

When you leave your job, your P45 should be returned to you. Make sure that it is, and keep it somewhere safe. You'll need it when you start your next job, and may need it to complete a tax return.

National Insurance

Your National Insurance (NI) number is unique to you and is a bit like a state identity number, used in all your dealings with the Inland Revenue and the government Department for Work and Pensions. It remains with you for your whole life and is used to pay tax and to record all your NI contributions (a nice way of saying another tax), which go towards state benefits. You'll need to quote it when you claim any kind of benefit – including your pension – and it's not optional. (Even if you have a private pension and never claim any benefit, you still have to pay NI.) You'll also need to give the number to your employer when you start work.

NB: your employer will automatically deduct NI contributions from your pay for you, but if you're self-employed you still need to pay NI and you are responsible for doing this. If you don't, you may have to pay a penalty, and/or lose some of your entitlements to state benefits. So call the Inland Revenue, ask for a P/SE/1 form, and they will very kindly send it to you, enabling you to pay.

Usually, when you start work, you should already possess a NI card with your number on it. However, if for some reason you don't, contact the Inland Revenue's NI department.

NB: you don't actually need the card itself, just the number, which you may be able to find by looking at old pay-slips or official documents (remember: your number never changes). But if you think it may have

been found by someone else, it's important to tell the Inland Revenue, so that no one else can use it pretending to be you.

You should also inform the Inland Revenue if there's any change to your name, address or title so that they know how to contact you if the need arises, and they can keep track of any benefits you're entitled to – beginning to sound like Big Brother, isn't it? For now, however, try to ignore the men in black, give the number to your employer, and get ready for the next system shock: paying tax.

Income tax

At the end of your very first month of work you will receive your very first pay-slip. It's a moment to savour and goes something a bit like this: pride (when it's handed to you); excitement (when you're opening it – but trying to pretend to be nonchalant because you're in the middle of the office and everyone else has done this a thousand times before); and then shock, horror, anger and disappointment (when you see the big, fat lump the taxman has deducted from your pay). And, as you realise that the taxman's share is almost as much as your own, all at once you develop an unprecedented interest in politics. Suddenly, you feel indignant that you're paying all this money and still the roads are rubbish and the buses don't work. And then another thought occurs: your pay-slip isn't as large as you thought it was, and you can't really afford to pay for those new boots.

Unfortunately, there's not a lot you can do, other than be aware from the start that as sure as the sun will rise, taxes will come – so factor them into your budget. The only up side is that for most people there's nothing you need to do personally to arrange payment of tax – your employer will do it for you.

Tax falls into different bands depending on how much you earn, and some people will be exempt. However, if your income falls into this tax-free category, you still have to pay tax, but will be able to claim it back (ask your local Tax Office for the relevant form, and find your local Tax Office by contacting the Inland Revenue). If you're a student, you're also exempt and can get your tax back by signing a Student Declaration Form (again, get this from the Inland Revenue). Alternatively, if you know in advance that your salary will be too small for you to pay tax, you can ask your employer for a special application form that will enable them to not make the deduction in the first place.

....

NB: the time limit for making a repayment claim is five years and 10 months from the end of the tax year in which you overpaid. The tax year runs from 6 April–5 April; however, all forms need to be returned to the Inland Revenue before 31 January of the following year.

....

If you're **self-employed**, or for some other reason need to be self-assessed, things become a whole lot trickier because you're going to have to fill in a more detailed Tax Return and figure the tax out for yourself, or return the form by the September prior to the January cut-off date for the Inland Revenue to calculate it for you. Contact the Inland Revenue who will advise you about the relevant forms. These come with an instruction booklet and if you are on PAYE are relatively simple – just make sure you include any other income such as shares or interest from savings. However, they are time-consuming. Be prepared to spend a LONG time filling them in. And remember also to keep a record of EVERY-THING (finally, an explanation as to why your dad always told you to keep receipts!).

Pensions – take heed of the squirrel

Now, if you're just starting work, retiring probably seems like a very long time away and a pension is probably the last thing on your mind. In fact, you're probably trying to scrape together enough of your salary to ensure that you can afford to live now, let alone putting money aside to finance your life later on. But, unfortunately, this is something you need to think about, as your state pension (the one you're putting all those NI contributions towards) is not going to get you very far.

Pensions can be either **contributory** or **non-contributory** and all companies are now legally obliged to offer employees some sort of pension scheme. A contributory pension means that the employer will put some money towards your pension each month, often matching whatever amount you contribute yourself. This is the kind of scheme you want to be on. A non-contributory pension, on the other hand, means you alone are making contributions, which will be deducted from your pay and go into a pension fund. However, all companies will offer different options, which may include a non-contributory pension as well as private health, or a contributory one with no other benefits, or a range of other options for you to choose from, so it's worth taking the time to work out what will best suit you.

If you're self-employed, there are still pension schemes open to you, but you will need to set up your own plan. To do this, talk to a financial advisor (at a bank, pension firm or independent investment company). They should then be able to look at your lifestyle and work out what kind of pension scheme is best.

....

NB: you do not have to join a pension scheme. Traditionally, these have been seen as vitally important, but after the run of very public pension debacles that have been in the media over the past few years, for many, pension schemes have lost a lot of their credibility. Many people now prefer to invest their money in

property, shares or other assets. This is completely up to you, but the important point here is to invest in something. Don't simply fritter your extra money away. Think ahead. Be like the squirrel. After all, tomorrow will come.

....

Trade unions – power to the people

When you start a new job, you might be asked to join a trade union. A trade union is basically a group of people in the same trade who join together to voice issues and protect each other's interests at work. A lot of industries have them and they can be great things to be a part of not only because they give your views much more clout but also because they will support you should you ever be involved in a dispute with your employer.

However, you do have to pay an annual fee, and, once a member, you are bound by decisions made about union activity – activity you might not necessarily agree with. So don't feel pressured to join. When you're new, it's easy to feel intimidated as you'll probably feel anxious to do what's asked of you and please your new colleagues. But you don't have to. And just as it's illegal for you to be victimised by your employer for deciding to join a trade union, it's also illegal for you to be victimised by your fellow workers for refusing. Take some time to work out what you want to do and then stick to your guns.

Rights and entitlements

This is the point where, unlike me in my first job, you stop yourself from being treated like a slave, and stand up to Hollywood producers should they start screaming at you. Most of your rights and entitlements should be laid out in your contract of employment, and will vary depending on the particulars you've agreed. For example, some companies will pay overtime, some won't. Some will expect you to be sitting at your desk bright-eyed and bushy-tailed at 7.00 a.m., whereas others won't bat an eyelid if you rock up at 10. Some will offer extra days off for Christmas shopping, whereas others will virtually expect you to work on Christmas Day. But regardless of what you have or haven't agreed to in your contract, there are some basic issues that all companies are obligated to uphold and are your greatest weapon with which to complain. They cover issues such as the minimum wage, working hours, holiday, study and dismissal, and you can get a full list of your entitlements from the Department of Trade and Industry.

Dismissal

This is the most likely time for things to turn sour. Unless agreed otherwise in your contract, you must give your employer a minimum of one week's notice before leaving your job. (Something to think about before you tell your boss where to go in your very dramatic, Bridget Jonesesque quitting speech – a week can seem like a very long time when working for a boss who hates you.) Similarly, your employer must give you at least one week's notice after one month's employment, two weeks' after two years, three weeks' after three years and so on up to 12 weeks' after 12 years or more.

You can be dismissed for a number of reasons that give your employer a pretty vague and all-encompassing ability to say confidently, 'Sorry, Charlie, you're sacked!' These reasons include: your conduct (for example, if you decide to turn up to work consistently at midday, tell the boss to f*** off, or secretly start growing a marijuana plant under your desk); your capabilities or qualifications for the job (like not having that C you said you had for GCSE maths and hence not being able to balance the books you promised you could balance); because your job has become redundant; and so on.

However, there are some reasons for dismissal that are automatically considered 'unfair'. These include: pregnancy or seeking to take maternity leave; seeking to take paternity leave; seeking to take parental leave (such as caring for a sick child) or other time off for dependants; taking certain types of health and safety action; refusing to do shop or betting work on Sunday; making a protected disclosure within the Public Interest Disclosure Act 1998 (that is, 'whistle-blowing': revealing secret information about the company because it's in the public interest to do so); asserting a statutory employment right (for example, demanding the minimum wage); trade union activities; demanding to be accompanied at a disciplinary or grievance hearing by a fellow worker – or being the person accompanying someone else.

....

NB: many other reasons for dismissal might appear to be 'unfair' to you; for example, you being fired for being consistently late when it was actually the train's fault, or you getting sacked for throwing a tantrum at the boss when it was obvious that you simply had your period! However, bear in mind that the courts might not see it the same way.

....

In any case, all complaints to be considered must be received by an employment tribunal within three months of termination.

If, however, you think that any of your rights have been infringed *before* you get fired, or you have any other concerns at work (bullying, for instance, doesn't stop with cat-calling in the playground), your first port of call should be your manager or human resources department. If they don't deal with the matter to your satisfaction, your next step should be to take the matter to an employment tribunal. If you're part of a trade union, they will be able to help you with this. If not, application forms for employment tribunals are available at JobCentres, Citizens Advice Bureaux, and employment tribunals themselves. However you go about it, the important point is DON'T put up with being abused or any of your rights being infringed. The law is there for a reason – now is the time to put *it* to work.

Hopefully, however, it won't get to that. Hopefully, you'll snag the job of your dreams, get paid lots of money, and, not too long from now, be the person doing the hiring and firing yourself, the person determining exactly which of the new working-world recruits will be lucky enough to follow your path. (Alternatively, you may spend two months working before deciding that early mornings are not the life for you, and you'd rather emigrate to a youth hostel in Mexico where you spend your time writing poetry and learning how to cruise the surf.) However, if all goes to plan and you do become a head honcho somewhere, try to remember what it was like to be a novice yourself. (And, while interviewing new candidates, if you happen to meet an out-of-work Hollywood movie producer – do me a favour: tell him that I'm still waiting for my cheque in the post.)

8
BANKING: SELL, SELL, SELL!

For most people, *making* money is the hardest part of finance; if someone offered me a million pounds, for example, I certainly wouldn't say no. However, *managing* money can be almost as tricky. I mean, let's just suppose that someone was kind enough to simply give me a million pounds (and let's just pause for a moment, little fingers poised Dr Evil style, to fully appreciate that).

OK, so now I've got a million pounds, what would I do with it? Obviously, the first thing I would do is go on a major shopping spree; but practically speaking, I couldn't lug a million pounds around in my purse, so where would I put it? Into what kind of account, and how would I open it? With which bank, and at what interest? How would I access it and what kind of card would I need? Should I invest in bonds? Or shares? And really, before we even start thinking about any of that, how would I bank the cheque in the first place (that is, assuming it didn't arrive in a briefcase full of unmarked fifties)?

For some people, (we'll call them 'Banker Geeks', or 'BGs' for convenience) the language of finance is like a lost language they were mysteriously born with, and these questions are all easily answerable. However, for others of the slightly more clueless variety, it was a bit of an achievement the first time we actually managed to make the ATM (cash machine) give us cash. In fact, I have a friend (who shall remain nameless) who owned a debit card for almost two years before she realised that she could actually pay for things with the plastic, instead of having to run down the road to withdraw cash every time she ran out of real money. And even now, having been 'banking' for years, I'm still not entirely certain if I'm writing everything I'm supposed to when filling out a cheque.

But the thing is, nobody ever showed us how. No one taught us how to write a cheque, or use a cash machine, or sign a credit card, and now this crazy chip-and-PIN thing is shaking up the world of personal finance – and still, no one has really shown us what to do.

So, having enlightened myself by talking to a myriad of BGs and doing endless research, here it is – here's what you need to know:

Banking Terminology

Before we can begin to understand the mysterious language of the BGs, it's essential that we cover a few of the most common terms used in BG-speak. Not all of these terms have an exact translation into normal English, but below is as close an explanation as I could find:

- **Account number:** this is your individual number that identifies your exact bank account. If you have more that one account, you will have more than one number. It can be found on your chequebook and paying-in book slips and on your bank statements.

  ....

  NB: your credit-card account does not operate in the same way as a normal account. Your card number (found across the middle of your card) acts as your account number instead.

  ....

- **Sort code:** this identifies both the bank you're with and the branch you're at. It can be found on the bottom left of your debit card, as well as on your chequebooks, paying-in books, and bank statements.

- **Security code:** this is an extra security measure to protect against fraud. It can be found on the back of your card, over the strip where you sign your name.
- **Interest rates:** these determine how much interest you will either gain (on your savings) or be charged (on your debts). They are set by banks themselves and are one of the main ways to distinguish between banks, but they are also dependent on the national rates set by the Bank of England.
- **Credit rating:** this is a score worked out to assess a person's ability to pay a debt. It analyses information such as previous debt repayment (whether it was slow or on time and if there were any defaults), current credit, income and assets (such as properties), amongst other factors. It's important because it affects what kind of account you can get at a bank, loan applications, mortgages, and so on. And it takes into consideration your complete history – the innocence of youth is not an excuse.
- **BACS (Bankers Automated Clearing Service) payments:** this is the method of transferring money from one account to another. It takes three days and is used to make direct debit and direct credit payments, as well as one-off transfers.
- **APR (Annual Percentage Rate):** this is the calculated cost of borrowing, taking into account interest

rates and other charges on a yearly basis. You will be told the APR when you apply for a loan.

- **ATM (Automated Teller Machine):** this is a cash machine where you can withdraw money.
- **Overdraft:** this is a buffer zone on your current account allowing you to spend beyond the amount of money you actually have, within a specified limit. In essence, it is a small loan from the bank and usually, unless you're a student, you will be charged interest.
- **'In the black/red':** you're in credit/debt (red for danger).
- **Bonds:** these are a form of low-risk/low-return, fixed-term investment. In essence, they are a loan from you to a company/the government, returned at a fixed rate of interest.
- **Stocks/shares:** these words are often used inter-changeably; they are basically a stake in the ownership of a company in which you will profit according to the company's success.

Choosing a bank

Most people join a bank for the first time when they're still a child, so the main factors tend do be: which one is located in your local high street and which one your parents belong to. This is not necessarily the most scientific way of choosing a bank. However, these factors shouldn't be discounted; you DO want a bank that is convenient to you and one that you can build a relationship with.

However, once you extend your banking transactions beyond that of a monthly deposit from your piggy bank, there are other things to consider too. For example, which bank will offer you the best rate of interest, which one will provide you with a debit or credit card immediately, what bank charges are there, and what extra services do they offer? The best way to decide is to do some research into a few different banks and find out which one is best suited to you. Unfortunately, this can be time consuming, but some websites will help make the comparisons for you. Building societies, which used to focus on savings rather than current accounts, now also usually offer current accounts, so these should be included in your search.

....

WARNING: banks tend to have big promotional offers to encourage you to bank with them: a free meal, discounted movie tickets, and so on. DON'T be fooled. These one-time offers are mere peanuts. You need to look to the long term. Focus on interest rates, not interesting bait.

....

Opening an account

Having a chosen a bank, you need to open an account. There are four basic types to choose from:

CURRENT ACCOUNT

This is the most common type of account for everyday banking and there's no minimum deposit necessary to open it. Usually it should include access to an overdraft, debit card, cheque guarantee card and chequebook. It gives you relatively small interest on your savings, but easy access, and usually there will be no bank charge to open it.

BASIC ACCOUNT

This is the most low-level account available and is generally given to people the bank considers to be dodgy – usually those with low credit ratings or those who can't provide enough proof of address to qualify for a current account. The aim here is to provide customers with the basic bank facilities (for example, cash cards and direct-debit facilities) but to limit the risk to the bank. Consequently, there are no credit facilities available, so no overdraft, and no chequebook.

PACKAGED ACCOUNT

These are still current accounts, so you can still have cards and chequebooks, and access your money in the same way. However, they're packaged to include extra benefits, such as discounted rates on mortgages and loans. They also throw in a special card, different from the basic current account, so the whole world can know just how special you are. These accounts however, are usually reserved for the, let's say, more valued customers, and there will generally be a bank charge attached, so it's worth it only if the savings from the extra benefits work out to be higher than that charge.

NB: if you're a really good customer you'll get an even more special card (the elusive American Express Black card, for example), and you'll get assigned your own personal bank manager to deal with all your transactions.

SAVINGS ACCOUNT

These are high-interest accounts. They give you a higher rate of interest because you usually have to give the bank a higher guarantee that you won't suddenly remove your money. You can still get a card for some of them, but the less access you need, the better rate of interest you'll get. There's usually a minimum deposit necessary and some bank charges.

NB: there are also a whole range of specialised accounts such as student and graduate accounts that offer incentives like interest-free overdrafts, business accounts and joint accounts, so make sure the bank explains its entire list of options.

To open an account, simply go into your chosen bank and tell them what kind of account you want to open. If, however, even after reading this, you still don't have a clue, tell the bank this, and someone will talk you though the various options. Of course, the choice of account is not entirely yours to make. The bank will assess your credit rating, income, and stability (such as proof of address) before allowing you set up an account. You will then be given credit only if the bank thinks you'll be able to repay it.

You will therefore need to provide most banks with: two forms of identification (typically a passport, driving licence or birth certificate) and a proof of address (such as your council tax bill or lease certificate). This is where some people struggle, as young people, especially students staying in university accommodation, don't always have the documents necessary to prove where they live. In some cases, banks will accept a letter of introduction from you, or a bank statement from a previous bank if you have one. However, if they don't, you probably won't get further than a basic no-credit account.

In all cases, the bank will then do a credit search and check for anything suspicious about your application such as different spellings of your name or opening an account far from where you live. However, assuming that you're not an arch criminal and you are approved, your account should usually become active that day, and you will receive your cards, chequebook, and other important details, within a couple of weeks. You will then become a fully-fledged member of the banking community – welcome.

....

NB: to close your account, simply go into the bank and tell them you want to close it. They might ask you a few probing questions as to why, make you feel guilty for leaving them, and try to tempt you back with news of their latest offers, but be strong – tell them it's not them, it's you, and that it would mean a lot to you if you could still be friends …

....

Online and telephone banking

You may have noticed that we've entered the 21st century. This means that technology is the order of the day. Telephone banking allows you to conduct a range of bank transactions over the phone, and can be set up simply by registering at your bank, but it's online banking that has revolutionised the world of personal finance because it means that you hardly ever have actually to go to the bank. In fact, with Internet shopping, cable TV and takeaways, if you can get someone to pay cheques in for you, you need never even leave your house! However, online banking does require a small amount of computer literacy, at least to get it set up, so if, for you, turning on a PC ranks alongside jumping out of a plane, it's probably better to stick with the good old-fashioned bank.

So, what are the benefits? Well, if not having to go to the bank and stand in a queue for half of your lunch hour isn't enough of a carrot, other advantages include: you can view your account online and track transactions (such as cheques in and out, and standing orders); you can pay bills (without having to write a cheque, fill in your account details, or write out your address for the hundredth time); you can set up direct debits and standing orders on your own; you can do it anywhere that there's a computer, at any time of day or night; *and* you save money on stamps. You can also shop around online to pick the bank that offers you the best interest and the best service.

However, there is a distinction to be made between traditional banks that now offer online services, and banks that exist only in the world of cyber-space. Essentially, they both offer similar services, but there are differences. Bricks-and-mortar banks will sometimes charge a small fee for Internet banking, whereas Internet-only banks won't – or at least the charges will be substantially less. Internet-only banks can also pass other savings on to you, because they don't have the running costs that traditional banks do. This will often materialise in lesser or even no fees, unlimited chequing, and so on. They may also offer more extensive online services. However, the bite-back comes in the form of ATM charges (because you'll have to use host machines), and the fact that without a real bank to make a deposit at you'll have to post your deposits, which can be time-consuming and less secure.

TO SET UP AN ONLINE ACCOUNT

If using a traditional bank, you should ask them for details of their online banking. They will then instruct you how to proceed. Generally, it will involve filling out a questionnaire and then triggering your account online (they'll give you a PIN for you to use and the web address you need to go to).

With Internet-only banks, the first thing to do is select the type of account you want to open, then fill out an application, which you print out, sign and post to the bank.

ONLINE SECURITY

As with many Internet transactions, security is the biggest drawback. It's less of a problem for bricks-and-mortar banks, but for the online-only variety, how do you know that the bank is a real bank and not a scam? How do you know that your money is safe? Well, to be honest, you don't. But there's a range of things you can do to protect yourself.

First of all, explore the bank's website. Is there a

phone number and contact address? If there is, call it and check that someone is actually at the end of the phone, then ask them some questions about the bank. (If there isn't a phone number – that's a pretty good indication that it isn't a proper bank.) There should also be a detailed explanation on the site about how the bank protects the security of your transactions; banks are aware of this issue as much as you are so they should address it. Most banks will use some kind of encryption for your transactions as well as other security measures. Make sure these are in operation when you're actually carrying out your transactions (a closed padlock icon should appear). And finally, make sure you are always asked for your PIN. If all these measures are followed, online banking should be safe.

Accessing your money

Some accounts (such as savings accounts and bonds) require you to give the bank a fixed period of notice before you can withdraw money. However, with most accounts, you'll be able to access your money immediately either at the bank, with a card, via a cheque or at an ATM.

AT THE BANK

For normal withdrawals, either use your debit card or give the cashier a cheque written to 'cash' for the amount you require. For large withdrawals (we're talking thousands here), you'll need to root around for your two pieces of ID again. And for really large withdrawals, you may need to give the bank some notice (a day or so – but again this is variable).

....

NB: banks generally close earlier than you would expect. Usually they're open until 5.00 p.m. Monday to Friday, and around 2.00 p.m. on a Saturday; but many banks will close at 4.00 p.m. on weekdays and 12.00 p.m. on a Saturday, so make sure you know what time the bank closes before waiting until the last minute to make that vital trip.

....

CARDS

Bank cards can be very convenient because they mean that you don't have to carry around huge wads of cash. They also enable you to pay for things over the phone and on the Internet. And some hotels and restaurants, for example, will require one as a guarantee to hold a reservation for you or against expenses you might incur. However, as with everything in life, not even a card is straightforward. There are four basic types of bank cards:

Cash-point card

These cards enable you to take money out of an ATM. You can't use it to buy anything (such as in a shop or restaurant), but you can withdraw cash. The bank will send you a PIN (Personal Identification Number) that you will need to remember in order to use your card.

....

NB: the first time you use your card you'll be asked if you want to change the PIN. If you find numbers hard to remember, it's a good idea to do this and make it something more memorable to you – but please, not your birth date; I know you're not James Bond, but, come on, make it a little bit difficult for people to guess!

....

Cheque guarantee card

This card can't be used in an ATM or in a shop. It acts merely as a guarantee to the retailer that your bank will pay the cheque that you are writing (up to a maximum amount that is shown on the card). Make sure you keep it with you, as the retailer should ask to see this card before accepting your cheque.

Debit card

This card allows you to pay money straight out of your current account in shops and restaurants, over the phone and on the Internet, without having to take the cash out of an ATM, although you can do this too. You can spend up to the amount you have in your bank, plus your overdraft.

To do this in the old days, you would simply show

this card to the retailer and sign the receipt they gave you. However, we have now entered the era of chip-and-PIN; introduced to increase card security, reduce fraud – and give us something new to negotiate. So, instead of signing (which is easier to forge than a secret number), you now have to type your PIN number into a small machine at the till.

....

NB: debit cards often act as a cheque guarantee card too.

....

Credit card

Evil master of the 'buy now, pay later' philosophy; treacherous founder of the 'spend more than you have' way of life; crafty creator of a thousand debts; and beloved facilitator of the spontaneous shopping spree: credit cards can be used to pay for things over the counter, on the phone and on the Internet, and are usually accepted anywhere in the world. However, credit cards are completely separate from your current account and do not involve any money you actually have. Instead, it is money the bank is prepared to lend you now to pay back later – with interest of course.

Each month, the bank will send you a statement with the minimum amount you have to repay (although it's advisable to pay more). This is generally a relatively small sum that you should be able to cope with – don't worry, they don't suddenly demand the whole lot back at once.

However, the longer you leave an amount outstanding, the more interest will accrue so that, ultimately, you end up repaying the bank far more than you ever spent – clever, huh?

So, while used wisely, the credit card can be a great liberator to your finances, allowing you to make your spending more flexible than if it was directly tied to your monthly income, if used flippantly, you can land yourself in debt. The best advice is to exert restraint. Don't take up every credit card you're offered, and remember: it's money you don't really have.

....

NB: different banks will offer different variations of each of these cards which may have slightly different functions, or embody more than one function on the same card. Just make sure you find out what your card can and can't do before you try to use it; it's very embarrassing to get to the front of a long queue only to be told that your card can't be accepted and you have to put everything back.

....

WARNING: Some shops will offer you **store cards** with the tempting offer of an immediate discount/free purchase/other distracting ploy. Beware. These cards act like credit cards, but usually charge a much higher rate of interest than banks, so your debt mounts up very quickly. Either pay the whole bill as soon as it arrives, or avoid these cards altogether.

....

NB: store credit cards are different from shop **loyalty cards** which can't be used to pay for goods, but offer rewards for your loyalty; they also offer the shop the chance to monitor your shopping habits – yes, I am a cynic – but if I were you, I'd reap the rewards while you can!

....

ATM (CASH MACHINES)

Operating an ATM for the first time is like having sex: there's a lot of fumbling around to start with, a lot of pressure, panic when you suddenly think you've done it all wrong, and then a great surge of happiness when you receive your cash (I'm talking about the ATM now, not prostitution). And once you realise how simple it is, and how great the rewards, you'll want to do it over and over again until you run out of money (still talking about the ATM – put away those dirty minds).

Seriously though, there's not a lot to it – but it can be intimidating if there's a whole queue of people impatiently waiting to use the machine and you arrive as an ATM virgin. So, here's what to do:

1. Put your card into the small (card-sized) slot in the machine (following the picture that shows you which way to insert it).
2. Key in your PIN when asked to do so.
3. Then simply read the instructions as they appear on

the screen and key in your answers. The questions will usually follow the lines of: choose your language; what service would you like to use; how much cash would you like; would you like another service.

And don't worry, they're not essay questions, they are all multiple choice so you can't really go wrong. However, if you do go wrong (if, for instance, you press the wrong button by mistake) there will usually be an option that says 'cancel'. Simply press this, ignore all the tutting people behind you, and try again. And if it really goes wrong (if, for instance, the machine eats up your card and tells you that you have no money), don't panic. Simply make a note of which ATM you were at, then go into your bank and explain to them what happened.

NB: you will usually have a maximum withdrawal limit stipulated for your account. This means that even if you have heaps of money in your bank, you will only be able to withdraw a certain amount from an ATM each day. Make sure you know your limit and go into the bank itself if you need a larger withdrawal.

CHEQUES

Without doubt cheques are the best way to send your money through the post, because if they're somehow lost or intercepted, they can be cancelled and stopped. They're accepted by most people and are good for transferring large sums of money. They also make it easy to keep track of your spending as, if filled out correctly, you should have all the information on your cheque stub. However, they are slightly more difficult to use than cash or card because they take a little bit of time to fill out, and they take a little bit of know-how:

1. Cheques can vary slightly from bank to bank, but most of them will look something like this:

2. To fill one out, begin by writing the name of the person/shop/company you are paying on the top line, after the word 'pay'.

3. Then, starting on the next line and using words, not numbers, write the full amount of money that you're paying, followed by the word 'only'. I know, when you're paying large sums of money 'only' doesn't quite seem appropriate but it's important to include

this so that no one can add anything to the end of the number you're writing. If it helps, think of 'only' as meaning 'and not a penny more'.

4. You now need to fill in the date (where it says 'date') either in number format (dd/mm/yy, for example, 29/08/05) or in full (for example, 29 August 2005), and then the amount you're paying (this time in numbers) in the box next to the £ sign.

5. Fill in the corresponding information on the cheque stub, make sure all the information on the cheque is correct, and then, as the last thing you do, sign the cheque.

....

NB: if you make a mistake at any point, simply cross out the mistake, put in the correction, and sign your initials next to it.

....

STANDING ORDERS

A standing order (SO) is set up by you at the bank. In essence, it's you giving the bank your authority to make a payment from your account to another account at a certain point, and usually at regular intervals such as monthly or annually. (It's useful for rent payments and deposits into your savings account, for example.) To set one up, you simply need to tell the bank and provide them with the bank details of the account the SO is going to.

DIRECT DEBITS

A direct debit operates in a similar way to a standing order, but it is an agreement between you and another person/company, rather than between you and the bank. To set this up, you need to sign a direct debit mandate, in which you will fill out your bank details. This gives the person/company the authority to make a claim on your account at a certain time (again, usually monthly, quarterly or annually, but it can be whenever costs occur).

BANKER'S DRAFT

For some of the bigger purchases in life such as cars and property you'll often find that cheques are not accepted. This is largely because they mean nothing until they are cleared, and the seller will want some guarantee that the money is actually there. So, unless you're planning on presenting the car dealer with a briefcase full of cash, you will need something called a banker's draft. In essence, this is a special cheque issued by your bank promising that you do have the money, the funds are clear and that your cheque will not bounce.

CHAPS PAYMENT

These are basically emergency payments. They enable you to transfer money from your account to another account by the end of business that day. As with banker's drafts, the bank will only transfer money that has already cleared in your account, hence, it is another secure way to send or receive funds. To arrange a CHAPS payment, simply call or visit your bank and tell them what you want to do. However, be aware that the bank will usually charge you for this service, so it's only worth doing if the transfer is substantial, otherwise, it pays to be organised.

BACS PAYMENT

This is the normal way to make a payment between accounts. It usually takes three days and can be arranged by simply asking your bank.

Paying money in

I know it's much more fun to take money out, but hopefully, at least some of the time, you'll be putting money into your bank too.

Money can be paid in in a variety of ways: by direct transfer or standing order (from another person/ company or from another one of your accounts), by cheque or cash at the bank itself, or now, in many places, even by ATM.

DIRECT TRANSFER/STANDING ORDER

To enable someone to transfer money directly into your account you will need to provide them with your account details. These generally include: your name (as it appears on your bank statements), the name of your branch, your account number and your sort code.

AT THE BANK

If you have either cash or a cheque that you want to pay into your account, you will need to go to the bank or you can send the cheque with a paying-in slip in the post. If you have a paying-in book, you can use this to pay your money in. If not, you can use the paying-in (bank giro credit) slips at the back of your chequebook, or a paying-in slip available from the bank.

The slips in your own chequebook/paying-in book are easier to fill out than the ones at the bank because they already have your bank details inserted. However, so long as you have your account details with you, even the bank ones are fairly easy to do:

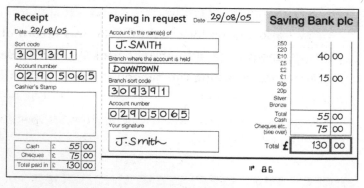

1. To fill out a slip, simply insert the date and your name (presuming you are the one paying the money in – although it doesn't have to be you), your account

number and sort code.

2. Now add the amount that you are paying in. This amount is broken down into different cash denominations, and also has a separate cheques category. This can be confusing. Breathe. All you have to do is write the total sum of money that you have in each denomination, or in cheques, next to the appropriate box and add it all up at the end.

3. If you have a lot of cheques, it can be a good idea to fill out the back of the slip as well. This is not obligatory, but it allows you to break down the deposit into individual cheques so that you have a record of each one. This is useful in case one of the cheques goes missing or you're later unsure whether or not it has been banked. Give the slip to the cashier or drop it in the box provided.

....

NB: it's also a good idea to keep your own record of banked cheques, as although the bank shouldn't lose their record, anything can happen.

....

4. Now just remember to fill out the paying-in slip stub and you're done – money banked.

Paying in money at an ATM

Many people don't yet realise it – and consequently stand in bank queues for hours – but many banks now offer the facility of paying money directly into the bank via an ATM. If your bank offers this, an option will appear on the ATM screen saying something along the lines of 'paying in'. If you select this option, the machine will then spit out an envelope, you enclose the cheques/cash, fill out the relevant details as you would a paying-in slip, and push the envelope through the slot provided. Job done.

Bank charges

This is one of those important things to look out for when choosing a bank and may not be explained in detail in the bank's literature. Most banks won't charge you for setting up a current account, or any of the other basic accounts. However, you will usually be charged for the packaged accounts that offer extra benefits. You may also be charged to use particular services, e.g. some banks will charge for ATM use.

The real bite of charges, however, comes when you owe the bank money. This varies from bank to bank, but charges can, for example, include: interest when you're in overdraft; a standard penalty charge if you go a penny over your overdraft limit; penalties for failing to make the minimum payment to your credit card account; unauthorised borrowing; card misuse; and unpaid direct debits.

The key is to respond to all charges promptly, and, even if you can't pay straight away, stay in communication with the bank so that they know what is happening and don't keep piling on the fees. Fail to communicate, and even the tiniest of bank charges can destroy your entire credit rating. For example, if you move to another country or go travelling for a while without informing the bank, they will continue to send correspondence to your old address and presume that you've received it. If, therefore, you're hit with a small bank charge, or an unexpected direct debit, even if it's just for a pound or two, and these go unpaid because you're away, the charges will begin to accrue. They can then spiral out of control with penalties and default notices, so that you return to find hundreds of pounds worth of bank charges, and an untouchable credit rating.

Money management

So, let's presume your credit rating is not untouchable, you've opened an account, you've got some money in the bank – now what? Well, you could invest in the right stock, hit it rich, watch your money go soaring and need to open a different account to maximise your interest. Or, if it doesn't go quite so swimmingly, you could run out of cash, run out of credit, and start pawning your great aunt's silverware. Hopefully, the latter will never happen. But even if you don't hit the big time, there's a lot you can do by managing your money – both at home and with the bank – to see it reach it's full potential. Let's start with the best scenario and presume, just for a minute, that things are going really well:

INVESTMENTS

If the bank notices a considerable amount of money in your account, suddenly you will become their best friend and they will automatically give you a ring just for a chat – and to ask if you'd like to invest it. Alternatively, you can approach them.

The four main forms of investment are:

1 High-interest savings accounts

These are like normal accounts but with less accessibility to your money, and consequently higher interest.

2 ISAs

These are high-interest accounts in which you don't have to pay tax on your interest. They are therefore a great way to invest, although there is a maximum amount of money you can put into each ISA. You also have to give the bank some notice before you take your money out.

3 Bonds

These are a form of low-risk/low-return investment. When you invest your money in a bond, you're giving a loan to a company/the government, who promise you a fixed amount of return for a fixed length of time. Because you're giving them the freedom to invest your money for a fixed period, you get a higher rate of interest than in a savings account. However, should you need to access your money before the fixed term is up, you'll be charged a penalty for removing your money early, which will affect your overall profits. There are of course variations within this; for example, some may be tied to the stock market and therefore carry greater risk.

4 Stocks and shares

These are tied to the stock market and are therefore a much more risky investment than bonds. However, they also have much greater potential. When you own a share or a stock you become a part owner of a company and receive a return on your investment depending on how well that company performs. It's a higher risk than a bond, as you get paid only after all the debtors have been paid, and the stock could actually decrease in value, but the potential to earn is limitless.

If you like, the bank will provide you with a financial advisor to help you decide what shares to invest in. Alternatively, you can use an independent advisor, go to a stockbroker, or make the gamble yourself.

....

NB: many people today prefer to invest their money in property. This can also be a risky venture, but is general-

ly more stable than the stock market, and often appeals because of its tangible nature – property being something you can actually see and touch, as well as own.

....

Of course, if your finances aren't going so well, there are other things to consider, and the first thing to do is draw up a budget.

BUDGETING

Sensible budgeting is basically the concept that you don't spend more than you earn. The best way to do this is to keep track of all your incoming and outgoing monies, and to make sure that the numbers match up. If they don't you'll need to reassess your outgoings and prioritise what is most essential.

A good way of starting a budget is to track your spending over the course of a month. Every day, note down exactly what money has come in, and what money has gone out (you may be surprised at how quickly the coffees at Starbucks can add up). If at the end of the month, you have money left over, congratulations, you are successfully living within your means. Now try to leave a little extra each month either for savings or for miscellaneous costs that may arise. However, if you find that you spent more money than you earned, and are edging further and further into your overdraft, it's time to bulldoze that budget.

The first thing to do is work out how much money

you have each month to spend. Then, use your sample month to make a list of all of the things you spend your money on. Put these items in order from the most necessary to the least (bearing in mind that a £100 pair of jeans may seem like a fashion essential, but it's not quite so essential as food, rent or heat). Now add up how much the absolute essentials cost. Hopefully, this will be less than the amount of money you have and you can simply start cutting the least essential items from your spending. However, if you find that your earnings can't even cover the basics, you'll need to seek further help; we'll deal with this in detail later, but overdrafts and loans can be a good temporary measure.

....

TIP: money tends to feel more real when you can actually touch it, making it more difficult to spend without guilt. So, if you find yourself getting a little swipe-happy with the debit card, set yourself a spending limit and take that money out of the bank in cash. Then, when you run out of cash, you know you have to stop spending.

....

OVERDRAFTS

One of the great advantages to keeping your money in a bank, rather than in a box under your bed, is that you can have access to money that isn't actually yours; in other words the beloved overdraft. And if you're struggling a little, an overdraft can be just the relief you need.

However, be careful that you don't start living on your overdraft. It's fine to use it to tide you through a tight spot, or to hold you until payday, but if it becomes something permanent, eventually you'll run out of overdraft, and then you'll be in serious debt.

To get an overdraft, or to extend an existing one (you'll be offered one when opening many current accounts), simply talk to the bank. The outcome, of course, will be dependent on your credit rating, your income and your length of custom.

LOANS

A loan can be essential to help you achieve something beyond your current financial capabilities – be it a car, a new business, or simply to keep you temporarily afloat. Banks aren't the only groups that give loans, but they're often a good place to start, and to get one you'll need to speak to your bank direct. They will of course assess your credit rating and your income, in order to help them work out whether or not you are a risk, so it's best to approach them before you start missing payments or doing anything that will affect your credit score.

Having been approved, the bank will then offer you different types of loans with varying options of how long you have to pay it back, at what interest, etc. Make sure you only agree to repayments that are genuinely within your means (otherwise you're just going to land yourself in a bigger pile of debt) and take the time to find the loan that's best for you. Of course, this might not be at the bank. There are a plethora of different companies who offer loans, often even for people with low credit ratings, so make sure you do your research. Some websites have been set up to help you.

WARNING: loan sharks are unlicensed lenders, operating illegally, who will offer you money when no one else will. Beware. They may seem like the answer if you are desperate, but they will charge very high interest (possibly forcing you to get a second loan to pay off the first), and they may turn mean if your repayments fall behind.

DEBT

Unfortunately, there are times when none of the above seems to work, and getting into debt can seem like a slow descent into a bleak abyss. Once the cycle begins, the walls get higher and higher, and the way out appears ever more distant. It doesn't have to be this way.

If you find yourself in debt, the first thing to do is identify it – I know, it sounds a bit self-helpy, but really, coming to terms with the fact that there's a problem is the first step to dealing with it. And the sooner you do this, the better chance you have of clawing your way out of the abyss.

Start by working out what the difference is between

your income and your expenditure, so that you know how much you can genuinely afford to pay out each month. Then, use your budget to make a prioritised list of all your necessary payments (you should already have cut anything unnecessary from your budget). The most essential items to pay are the ones that carry the biggest consequences if you don't: the ones that can send the bailiffs around to repossess your home, take away your furniture, cut off your water, gas and electricity, or even land you in prison. Don't panic, the mortgage company won't suddenly appear with a SWAT team in tow because you were two days late on your mortgage payment. There will always be some warning, but you may need to act quickly, and the mortgage company is probably the most urgent.

The first thing to do is *communicate*. Contact all of your creditors in order of urgency, and explain your situation. Do this in the first instance with an informal phone call in which you can even ask for their advice. They may talk things through with you on the phone or ask you to meet with them to discuss your options. If you meet with them, it's a good idea to take a copy of your personal budget listing all your debts and how much you're offering to each creditor. This shows them exactly how much you can afford, and is evidence of your sincerity in trying to pay the debt. If you don't meet with them, send them a copy of your budget in the post. You should then make a new offer of repayment at a rate you can afford and ask them to freeze the interest on your debt.

NB: **this interest freeze is the most beneficial element to renegotiate, if you can. Unless your repayments are larger than the interest you're being charged, your debts will continue to grow, so the only way to get out of the cycle is to increase your payments, or to reduce the interest you pay.**

Hopefully, the creditor will respond with understanding. Your offer may be below what they were expecting, but generally it's in their interest for you to be able to make the repayment. So, with a bit of luck, they'll agree to your new offer and you can adjust your personal budget accordingly before contacting the next creditor.

Credit debts (such as bank loans, overdrafts and credit cards) are less urgent, although they still carry weighty consequences and so the creditors should still be contacted as soon as possible. Treat these in the same way as your other creditors.

WARNING: **some banks may panic at the idea of a big debt and clear your current account in order to cover your debt on your credit card. Usually this will not happen, and in fact the bank may be able to offer valuable help in the form of advice or consolidation loans (putting all your debts together so that you have just**

one monthly repayment), but you might want to consider opening a current account for your income at another bank, just in case.

Personal loans should be treated in the same way as other creditors; although, hopefully, your friends won't try to repossess your house. Companies, however, won't look kindly on you repaying large chunks of personal loans if you're paying off your debt to them in only small amounts. So, talk to your friends or family and try to negotiate some kind of repayment over a fixed term.

NB: the Citizens Advice Bureau can offer further advice on dealing with debt.

RECORDS

Whether you are in debt or making millions, keeping records of your finances is essential. It's not just a matter of knowing where to find the receipt for the shirt that doesn't fit, or for the toaster that broke, it's about collecting evidence to prove where your money has gone. Sometimes, you might simply be proving it to yourself, but at other times you might need to show this evidence to the Inland Revenue to pay your tax, to creditors, or even to courts. You might also need to consult previous bank statements to check whether or not certain bills have been paid, or to make sure there's been no unauthorised spending on your account, so keep these too.

....

NB: always check your bank statements, as mistakes can be made.

....

Keeping track of your spending in this way also means that you should always have an accurate overview of your financial situation, and not find yourself stranded on a remote island in the middle of nowhere when you debit card is cut up by a smug shop assistant.

Travelling: some dos and don'ts

There's no denying it – the world has got smaller. Even some of the most remote places on Earth have Internet connections and ATM machines, so the hazards of banking when abroad are now far fewer than they used to be. However, there remain a few travelling dos and don'ts to be aware of:

- Order your traveller's cheques from the bank at least a couple of days in advance of your travel – they are much safer to carry around than cash.
- Order your currency in advance also – you're likely to get a better exchange rate at the bank than at the airport.
- Most debit cards will work in most ATMs around the

world, but try to limit this, as you'll be charged a hefty fee for using a foreign ATM.

- Credit cards are usually accepted everywhere, as are Maestro debit cards; however, some cards will not be accepted, so find this out before you travel.
- If you're going to be away for a long time, inform your bank so that you won't be caught out by unpaid bank charges.

And finally ... enjoy. By now, you should be a fully-fledged, completely competent, sharp-as-a-knife member of the international banking community. You should even be able to pass yourself off as a Banker Geek. Show it off. And if, on your travels, you meet an actual BG, smile knowingly, then ask them about the stability of interest rates, the rise of online banking and the state of their shares.

9
OTHER STUFF YOU SHOULD KNOW

There are some things in life that don't fall into distinct categories. You might know nothing about banking, for example, but at least it's a proper topic. It's something you're aware that you know nothing about, and you can read the banking chapter in this book to fill you in. However, there are certain issues that you don't realise you're clueless about until they suddenly hit you, bang in the middle of some regular Thursday afternoon. They're the things that leave you reeling, suddenly feeling like a kid in disguise. But never fear. Below, are a whole range of issues that you might otherwise be faced with unarmed, and enough advice to help you sail though seamlessly.

Death and taxes

Benjamin Franklin said that nothing in life was certain, except death and taxes. Well, he was almost right, but birth is pretty certain too (although I guess we don't really remember much of our own birth), and it's likely that at some stage, a lot of people will get married. Now we've already dealt with taxes, but what do we do when one of these other probabilities occur? I mean, it's one thing to say, 'I do', but an entirely different thing to know what to do.

The first thing to work out is where your local register office is located, as this will be necessary to know for births, marriage and death. You can find this out either by searching on your county council's website, or by looking in your local phone book. You're now ready to go. (The following information was gleaned from the General Register Office.)

BIRTH

When you have a baby, after a few hours of cooing over it, you must register the birth. This has to be done within 42 days, either at the local register office, or often it's possible at the hospital itself. If you're married, either one of the parents can register the birth. If not, the mother has automatic parental responsibility. (However, if the father acts with her at registration, he acquires parental responsibility too.)

Registration takes about half an hour, and most offices operate an appointment system, so phone ahead to check. You don't need to take anything with you as the hospital should have notified the registrar of the birth, but it's helpful if you can take the mother's hospital discharge summary. You'll also need to know: the time and date of birth; the intended names of the child; the sex of the child; the mother's personal details and the father's details if he is to be included on the register; as well as the details of your marriage (if you're married).

You will then be asked to check the information; do this carefully as it's difficult to change at a later date and you don't really want little Steven to be forever known as 'Stewed' because of an innocent typo. You'll then be given one birth certificate free of charge and will be able to buy an extended version (like the DVDs with extra features), as well as extra copies if you want them.

If you ever need to replace a birth certificate, you can phone the register office, or apply online: www.gov-certificates.co.uk.

MARRIAGE

The first thing to do after saying 'yes' is to decide where

you want to get married. (Actually, this is the first *official* thing you have to do. Before that, you will probably want to par-tay!)

You can be married in a church, another religious building, or in a civil ceremony, but the processes for each are slightly different:

Anglican church

This is the marriage that requires least documentation, but it does require a conversation with the vicar. You must speak to the vicar of your local parish and ask him to marry you. If he agrees, he'll arrange for the banns to be called, or for a common licence to be issued. You don't usually have to involve the registrar.

Other religious buildings

As with the Anglican church, in other denominations or religions, you must also speak to the rabbi/cleric/Jedi knight in charge of marriages at the religious building in question. However, this building must be registered for marriage, and will usually have to lie in the registration district in which you or your partner lives. You'll also have to give the superintendent registrar formal notice of your marriage and complete all the civil preliminaries (explained below).

NB: you can get married in a religious building outside your district, or in a religious ceremony not in a certified religious building (your garden, for example), but you will need to have a civil ceremony also.

Civil preliminaries and ceremony

To make things legal, you must give the superintendent registrar notice of your marriage at least 16 days before the marriage can take place – at a small cost (yes, not even love is free). Your notice will include your names, ages, address(es), occupations, nationalities, marital status and the intended venue for the marriage, so you will need to provide documentary evidence of all of these. The notice is displayed at the register office for the 16 days, after which you have 12 months in which to tie the knot.

You can then either have a civil ceremony at the register office, or a religious or civil ceremony with an attending registrar somewhere else.

Once hitched, you'll be given your marriage certificate immediately after the ceremony, so make sure that you either pay in advance or that your wedding dress/tux 'n' tails has a pocket (!)

If you need to replace a certificate, you can do so either via the register office or online.

NB: the minimum legal age for marriage in the UK is 16, but written consent from a parent or guardian may be necessary for anyone under the age of 18.

DEATH

When someone dies, the last thing you want to think about are legalities. However, deaths must be registered within five days and the medical certificate with cause of death must be taken to the register office. Of course, if someone has died outside hospital, the first thing you should do is call a doctor or an ambulance, not hurry off to the registrar; besides, a doctor may well do the registration for you (make sure you ask him if he's going to). However, once this has been done, and if the doctor doesn't register the death, you must do it quickly as the funeral can't take place without it.

NB: most deaths are registered by relatives of the deceased, but a doctor, the person making the funeral arrangements, or anyone who was present at the death can do it. If a coroner is involved (for example because the death is suspicious, because no doctor was seen, or because the cause of death is unknown), the death cannot be registered until the coroner has completed his investigation.

You must then arrange for the removal of the body. If you don't know any undertakers, you can find one in the Yellow Pages. However, there may be a particular religious body or undertaker that you may prefer or that family or friends will suggest. You will also need to think about where you want the burial or cremation to take place. If you're a member of a church/synagogue/mosque/ and so on, the staff there should be able to give you advice. Otherwise ask the undertaker or local authority for help.

You can buy a death certificate, if you want one, as soon as the death has been registered, or you can get one from the local register office at any time within the next 18 months, or from the Family Records Centre after that. The registrar will also issue a certificate for the burial or cremation of the body. If the coroner is involved, he will often issue such a certificate so that the funeral is not delayed. You should pass this certificate on to the funeral director where you have chosen to have your funeral.

Unfortunately, there follows more paperwork. You need to fill out a certificate so that the Department for Work and Pensions can sort out what happens to the deceased's benefits, execute the will, etc. And the registrar will give you a 'What to do after death' booklet, which gives advice about probate and other administrative issues.

Voting

In case you hadn't noticed, you live in a representative democracy – at least that's what they tell us – and that means that you get to vote. This is a right that blood has been spilled over for centuries and is your only opportunity to let the people in power know what you think, or at least for that thought to make a difference. So, do your research, get an opinion, and be counted.

Anyone who is over the age of 18, and is either British, or a member of another Commonwealth country and has British residency, can vote. Foreign nationals in the UK, sentenced prisoners, some mentally ill patients, and members of the House of Lords can't vote, but everyone else can. British citizens can even vote when overseas, so long as they haven't been abroad for more than 15 years.

However, before you rush to the polls, you first need to be registered on the electoral roll in your area. Usually, the council will send you a registration form, which you simply need to fill in and return to them. However, if for some reason you've been missed out (or if you forgot to return the form), you can register by contacting your local authority and asking for a form, or by filling one out online.

On election day itself, all you need to do is go to one of your local polling booths, and put an X in the right box – simple. In the run-up to the election, there will probably have been signs posted all over the place, and leaflets stuffed through your door telling you exactly where you can vote (usually at local schools, town halls, and so on). However, if you don't know where to go, call up your local authority and ask them.

NB: you can now also vote by post if this is more convenient. However, you'll need to register in advance to do so. Download the form (see Useful Contacts for address) or get it from your local authority.

Once at the polling station and staring at your voting slip, you might be surprised to discover that the names on the piece of paper are not those of the PM and his or her opposition. And you might find that you don't have a clue who the people listed actually are. Don't worry, you have not suddenly woken up from amnesia and missed the last 20 years of politics. The names listed are your *local* candidates for each party, instead of the leaders. Because of our simple plurality voting system (also called first-past-the-post), and the fact that our democracy is *representative*, each local area votes for the local candidates they are presented with, rather than the leaders of the parties, or just a party in general. Then, the party that has the most local candidates elected forms the national government. So, if you haven't done any research into what your particular local candidates are about (which, by the way, it might be a good idea to do), simply pick the candidate who is from the party that you support. Then, drop your voting slip into the ballot box, and that's it. Congratulations. You have successfully participated in the democratic system and contributed to the political history of our country.

Passport

Look after your passport. It's important. You will need it whenever you travel abroad, and it may also be required as ID for a whole variety of reasons, such as to get a driving licence, bank account and mortgage. Most people know this already. However, what you might not know if you're an adult-novice, is that you are responsible for renewing it – yes, a passport runs out. Some countries even require that it be valid for a chunk of time (six months or so) after your date of travel before they will let you enter the country. So, keep an eye on your expiry date, and remember to apply to the UK Passport Service (UKPS) for a renewal well in advance of needing it.

To do this, you need: an application form, your current passport, two identical passport photos (of yourself) and payment. You can apply a maximum of nine months before your old passport runs out. If, however, your passport has been lost or stolen, you obviously need to replace it straight away, and you will need to fill in a lost passport form (to help the authorities stop someone passing themselves off as you).

NB: if your passport is lost or stolen while you're abroad, contact the local police and the nearest British Embassy, who will advise you.

If you have any questions about how to fill any of this in, want to make an appointment, or if you have any other questions about passports, call the Passport Service's Adviceline.

Passport applications usually take about two weeks to be processed, but there could be a delay, especially during the busy holiday season. If you don't need the renewal urgently, you can make the application by post or at a high street partner (selected Post Offices and Worldchoice travel agents). However, if you need it in less than two weeks, you'll need to go to one of the seven UKPS offices: Belfast, Durham, Glasgow, Liverpool, London, Newport or Peterborough. Make an appointment before you go, then use the Premium (one-day) or Fast Track (one-week) service, which demand a higher fee. However, appointments aren't guaranteed, as there are a limited number each day, so you may need to employ a few well-timed tears. Also, remember to take all important documents with you, as you may need to prove your identity, address, and so on.

The Post Office

As well as handling everything to do with mail, the Post Office also deals with: banking; benefits and pensions; foreign currency; phone cards and mobile top-ups;

licences: TV, driving, fishing, and so on ... and it's worth trying them for other things too.

Bar banter

You'll only be naive once and you may well have passed this stage years upon years ago. If you haven't, perhaps this is one area that's best left untaught. However, I remember my first trip to a bar, when I was first asked by the boy I was dating what I would like to drink – and I remember that I would have liked some help. Now, it must be said that I was underage – come on though, weren't we all? So I hadn't had much experience in drinking (in fact, it was limited to a bottle of Malibu that a friend had once tipped into our McDonald's Cokes, and the kosher wine we sipped on Shabbat). But this was even more reason to try not to sound stupid. Of course, my mind went blank. The only drinks I could think of were wine or beer, but I wanted to sound cooler than that. And suddenly I remembered the name 'whisky'. 'Inspiration!' I thought and ordered a whisky with ice. The barman laughed, so did my date, and I spent the whole evening trying not to cough the drink back up. So, if you don't want to stick with beer or wine, here's a quick list of some of the cooler cocktails to order – at least until you find out what you really like:

- Bellini (champers and peach – very classy, darling)
- Black Russian (for the sweet-toothed)

- Bloody Mary (add extra Worcester sauce for a bit of extra kick)
- Caipirinha (a tangy Latin-American classic)
- Cosmopolitan (for all Carrie Bradshaw wannabes)
- Flaming Lamborghini (only for the hard core)
- Gin and tonic (aka 'G and T')
- Margarita (salt around the rim – looks like a proper cocktail)
- Mai Tai (sweet and smooth)
- Martini (the drink of 007 – what could be cooler?)
- Mojito (the 'j' is a 'hch' sound – it's Cuban, baby!)
- Sea Breeze (you can almost hear the waves)

Casino courtesy

So, you're all dressed up, you've bought your chips, you're up for a great night of gambling – now what do you do? Well, if you're one of those people who are automatically comfortable in the chic danger of underworld, with roulette wheels and poker tables penetrating your consciousness almost from birth, you don't need me to tell you. If, however, you feel more comfortable with flapjacks than blackjack, and think that Rummy is just a drink – never fear. While I can't promise to teach you how to gamble properly, I can, in a matter of paragraphs, tell you how not to look silly in a casino.

OK – the first rule is to keep it simple. You're not going to become a poker hound overnight, and remember: we're only trying to make you *look* like a casino regular, not actually turn you into one. So, let's concentrate on the aesthetics:

1. The first thing to do before you sit at a table is to check the signs for the minimum bet per hand. (The table that says £1,000 minimum is probably not where you should start – unless you are a millionaire and a firm believer in beginner's luck.)
2. Having sat down, place your chips on the table in front of you, but not in the betting box, otherwise they could be mistaken for a bet.
3. Pick up your cards with one hand only, always keeping the cards above the table.
4. To get another card: tap the table (lightly – you won't be popular if you send all the cards flying), beckon to the dealer with your finger, or, if you're holding the cards, rub the left edge of the cards on the table felt.
5. To refuse another card, wave your hand over your cards (if they're on the table), or, if you're holding them, tuck them under the chips you've bet.
6. If you run out of chips while at a table, the dealer can change up more chips for you. However, DON'T try to hand him or her the money. This is simply not casino etiquette. You must put the money on the table so that everyone can see that nothing dodgy is going on. Then the dealer will pick the money up and give you your chips.

The easiest games to try your luck at are probably blackjack (a sophisticated version of pontoon or 21 – basically you're trying to get your cards to add up to 21), or roulette (you bet that the wheel will land on a number or group of numbers). Alternatively, the slot machines are fairly self-explanatory – just make sure you get one that's primed, and try not to get duped by the fantasy that the next one will *definitely* pay off.

You should now be able to look like a true gambler. Bet with confidence. And if anyone asks you to play anything complicated, simply smile knowingly and say something like, 'Nah, I'm not wearing my poker underwear tonight...' – all gamblers respect superstition.

Sounding smart

The final key to surviving in the 'real world' is *sounding* like you belong there. Once an adult, you're suddenly expected to sound clever and be interested in all manner of current affairs that you may find you know very little about. It was different at school. There you could be sporty, or theatrical, or arty, and that was your thing. You could say, 'I'm not really into politics', without an eyelid being batted. But now the same answer makes you sound like an uncultured, uncivilised, uneducated brute. So, here's a very brief list of phrases that should get you through even the toughest of political inquisitions:

'It's all a question of whether the ends justify the means.'

Seriously, this works, try it out. For example:

- 'What do you think of the Iraq war?'
  'Well, it's all a question of ...'
- 'Can you believe the goverment are going to put up income tax?'
  'Well, it's all a question of...'
- 'Should we set up harsher laws on immigration?'
  'Well, ...' See where I'm gong with this?

'That's democracy for you ...'

This is a phrase for the cynical, but it also makes you sound like you have a great grasp on the overall picture, and saw this coming years ago. For example:

- 'Have you heard about that new security law?'
  'Yep, that's democracy for you.'
- 'Did you see the huge protests before the war?'
  'Yep, that's democracy for you.'

'The problem is the extremists on both sides.'

Appropriate for discussions about any conflict. For example:

- 'Do you think the new [insert appropriate nation] PM will be any good?'
  'He may well be, but the problem is the extremists on both sides.'
- 'Do you think there's much hope for a stable [insert troubled nation]?'

'I don't know, the problem is ...'

The trick is to use each phrase at the right time, but do it confidently and you'll sound like you're completely clued up. Plus, the chances are that the person you're talking to is just trying to sound good too, so the vaguer your answer, the more likely they are to presume you know what you're talking about and leave it alone. Alternatively, you could read the newspaper and actually form an opinion of your own.

So, you can now sound like you're a proper adult, and, hopefully, this chapter will have picked up on enough of the loose ends that you can act like one too. However, by no means is it an exhaustive process. There will always be things that we don't know how to do, and situations that throw us onto the back foot – it's a fool who believes they know everything. The fun, of course, is in the learning – and then tutting smugly when you notice someone else making the same mistakes.

However, don't tut too loudly, because if, on the off-chance, this book has missed anything, you might all at once find yourself feeling like a novice again, your inner-kid revealed, and, suddenly, not so mature and independent. Don't despair – they say 30 is the new 20, and 40 is the new 30, so at this rate, we'll be 100 before we really have to grow up.

10
USEFUL CONTACTS

BANKING AND MONEY
Comparing bank accounts
Websites:
www.support4learning.org.uk/
   money/banks_tips.htm (great
   for students and young
   people),
www.news.ft.com/your money
www.fairinvestment.co.uk

Comparing loans
Websites:
www.moneysupermarket.com
www.onlyloans.co.uk
www.easy-quote.co.uk
www.AdviceOnline.co.uk
www.bonaportdirect.co.uk/
   cheapest-loan

GENERAL ADVICE
Citizens Advice Bureau
Citizens Advice
Regional Office
11 Upper Crescent
Belfast, BT7 1NT
Tel: 028 90 231120
Website:
www.citizensadvice.co.uk

HEALTH
Association of Optometrists
61 Southwark Street
London, SE1 0HL
Tel: 020 7261 9661
Website:
www.assoc-optometrists.org

British Dental Association
64 Wimpole Street
London, W1G 8YS
Tel: 020 7935 0875
Website:
www.bda-dentistry.org.uk

British Medical Association
BMA House
Tavistock Square
London, WC1H 9JP
Tel: 020 7387 4499
Website: www.bma.org.uk

Dental advice
Websites:
www.dentalhealth.org.uk/helpline
www.beyondfear.org

Family Planning Association
2-12 Pentonville Road
London, N1 9FP
Tel: 0845 310 1334
Website: www.fpa.org.uk

Medical advice
Website: www.surgerydoor.co.uk

National Health Service
NHS Direct
Tel: 0845 4647
Website: www.nhsdirect.nhs.uk

NHS Patient Services (Benefit
Inquiry)
Tel: 0845 850 1166

NHS 24 (Scottish Advice Line)
Tel: 08454 24 24 24

HOME IMPROVEMENTS
The Association of Building
Engineers
Billing Brook Road
Weston Favell
Northampton, NN3 8NW
Tel: 0160 440 4121
Website: www.abe.org.uk

Association of Plumbing and
Heating Contractors
14 Ensign House
Ensign Business Centre
Westwood Way
Coventry, CV4 8JA
Tel: 024 7647 0626
Website: www.aphc.co.uk

The Federation of Master
Builders
Gordon Fisher House
14-15 Great James Street
London, WC1N 3DP
Tel: 020 7242 7583
Website: www.fmb.org.uk

The Guild of Builders and
Contractors
Crest House
102-104 Church Road
Teddington
Middlesex, TW11 8PY
Tel: 020 8977 1105
Website:
www.buildersguild.co.uk

Royal Institute of British
Architects
66 Portland Place
London, W1N 4AD
Tel: 020 7307 3700
Website: www.ribafind.org

Royal Institute of Chartered
Surveyors
RICS Contact Centre
Surveyor Court
Westwood Way
Coventry, CV4 8JE
Tel: 0870 333 1600
Website: www.rics.org

INSURANCE
Association of British Insurers
51 Gresham Street
London, EC2V 7HQ
Tel: 020 7600 3333
Website: www.abi.org.uk

Comparing car insurance
Websites:
www.search4u.biz no
www.motorquotedirect.co.uk
www.4insurance.co.uk

Health insurance
Websites:
www.quotations.healthinsurance
  group.co.uk
www.preferredmedical.co.uk

MOTORING
Department for Transport
Great Minster House
76 Marsham Street
London, SW1P 4DR
Tel: 020 7944 8300
Website: www.dft.gov.uk

Driving Standards Agency
Stanley House
56 Talbot Street
Nottingham, NG1 5GU
Tel: 0115 901 2500
Website: www.dsa.gov.uk

Driver and Vehicle Licensing
  Agency (DVLA)
Customer Enquiries
  (Drivers/Vehicles) Group
Sandringham Park
Swansea, SA7 0EE
Tel: 0870 240 0009 (drivers)
    0870 240 0010 (vehicles)
Car Checking Service Tel: 0906
  185 8585
Website: www.dvla.gov.uk

Speed camera spotters
Websites: www.roadangel-
  direct.com
www.snooper.co.uk.

The UK Police Service
Website: www.police.uk

Vehicle Certification Agency
  (VCA)
1 The Eastgate Office Centre
Eastgate Road
Bristol, BS5 6XX
Tel: 0117 9524235
Website: www.vca.gov.uk

Vehicle and Operator Services
  Agency (VOSA)
Berkeley House,
Croydon Street,
Bristol, BS5 0DA
Tel: 0870 6060440
Website: www.vosa.gov.uk

WORK
Department of Health
Richmond House
79 Whitehall
London, SW1A 2NL
Tel: 020 7210 4850
Website: www.dh.gov.uk

Department of Trade and
  Industry
DTI Response Centre
1 Victoria Street
London, SW1H 0ET
Tel: 020 7215 5000
Website: www.dti.gov.uk

Department for Work and
  Pensions
Room 112
The Adelphi
1-11 John Adam Street
London, WC2N 6HT
Tel: 020 7712 2171
Website: www.dwp.gov.uk

JobCentres
Tel: 0845 6060 234
Website:
www.jobcentreplus.gov.uk

Job search sites
Websites:
www.jobsearch.co.uk
www.jobsite.co.uk
www.milkround.com (good for
  graduates)

Recruitment and Employment
  Confederation
36-38 Mortimer Street
London, W1W 7RG
Tel: 020 7462 3260
Website: www.rec.uk.com

TAX
HM Customs and Excise
Tel: 0845 010 9000
Website: www.hmce.gov.uk

Inland Revenue
NI Department
Tel: 0845 915 7006
Tax Credits
Tel: 0845 300 3900
Website:
www.inlandrevenue.gov.uk
Tax Credit Helpline
Tel: 0845 609 5000

TRAVELLING
The UK Passport Service
Passport Services Adviceline tel:
  0870 521 0410
Passport Application tel: 0901
  4700 110
Website: www.ukpa.gov.uk

UTILITIES
British Services (Directory of all
  British Services)
Website:
www.britishservices.co.uk

Comparing utility suppliers
Websites:
www.ukpower.co.uk
www.energyhelpline.com

British Telecom
Tel: 0800 443 31
Website: www.bt.com

The Energy Information Centre
Rosemary House
Lanwades Business Park
Newmarket
Suffolk, CB8 7PW
Tel: 01638 751400
Website: www.eic.co.uk

VOTING
Website:
www.aboutmyvote.co.uk

INDEX